HISTORY AND CHARACTER

OF

AMERICAN REVIVALS

OF

RELIGION.

AMS PRESS

NEW YORK

HISTORY AND CHARACTER

OF

AMERICAN REVIVALS

OF

RELIGION.

BY THE

REV. CALVIN COLTON,
OF AMERICA.

LONDON:

FREDERICK WESTLEY, AND A. H. DAVIS.

MDCCCXXXII.

Library of Congress Cataloging in Publication Data

Colton, Calvin, 1789-1857.
    History and character of American revivals of
religion.

    1. Revivals--U. S.   I. Title.
BV3773.C6 1973   269'.2'0973   72-10(
ISBN 0-404-00018-5

13119

Reprinted from the edition of 1832, London
First AMS edition published in 1973
Manufactured in the United States of America

AMS PRESS INC.
NEW YORK, N. Y. 10003

TO

BRITISH CHRISTIANS,

THIS VOLUME

IS

RESPECTFULLY DEDICATED,

BY

THE AUTHOR.

ERRATA.

On page 80th, 7th line from the top, for—*of course*—read—*in all cases.*
Page 187, 3d line from the top, for—*pantheism*—read—*Heathenism.*
Page 208, 6th line from the top, for—*as to reserve*—read—*yet reserving.*

CONTENTS.

INTRODUCTION.

THE publication of this little volume may
perhaps demand an apology. And it is
hoped by the Author, that it may seem as
reasonable, as it is simple. Soon after his
arrival in London, he received a note from
an esteemed and reverend brother, re-
questing him to deliver a discourse in his
chapel on *American Revivals*. The Author
answered the note, that he would take the
request under consideration. The demand
was altogether unanticipated, the topic
delicate, and difficult of treatment before
a popular assembly,—but yet interesting,
and so far as the Author could learn, important in the eyes of British Christians;
as the religious public in England were
yet in suspense, as to the opinion proper
to be entertained on the subject, on account

of the vague, unconnected, and indistinct reports respecting it. A general historical narrative, comprehending particulars, was out of the question, as the Author was altogether unfurnished with the necessary documents. He however consented, and occupied two separate occasions, and part of a third, in the same Chapel. He was requested to deliver the substance of the same discourses in other Chapels of the metropolis, and of the country, and has done so. And he has reason to be grateful for the kindness with which they have been received, for the interest manifested, and would humbly hope, that the attempt, however unsatisfactory to himself, may be of some service to the cause. The substance of those discourses having been in several instances requested for the press, it finally resulted in a consent, that some thoughts on the general subject, in a different form, should appear before the public in a Tract by itself, instead of taking the medium of a periodical. And the

Author was the more willing to do so, because, notwithstanding the approbation many had been pleased to express of what he had already done, he himself felt, and honestly felt, that it was not *the* thing. After it was too late to retreat, he found it was impossible to do anything like justice to the subject from the pulpit. Public attention, in a promiscuous congregation, assembled for an hour, could not be claimed for a naked historical narrative, even if the Author himself had been furnished with the necessary items. A discussion of principles was also discouraging. And a few insulated anecdotes would evidently be a very inadequate representation to those, who were strangers to the scenes, from which they might be selected. And, although what was actually done, was kindly received, the Author himself was obliged to feel, that, if he could have appreciated beforehand the difficulties of the task, he should certainly have shrunk from it. He

cannot honestly say, that he has unalloyed
satisfaction in the retrospect,—and that,
because he is deeply conscious of the unavoidable imperfections of the endeavour.

There is another embarrassing fact in
such a case :—The reports of American
Revivals have very naturally and inno-
cently raised somewhat of extravagant
expectation on this side of the Atlantic.
And it is impossible to satisfy that expectation—not for want of facts, of historical
verities—but on account of current mis-
conceptions. The expectation seems to
demand of us Americans, who have been
in the midst of these scenes, ' Show us a
sign from heaven.' But that is impossible.
And then there is danger of a falling-off
into the hasty conclusion, ' It is nothing
after all.'

The Author has also ascertained, since
he had actually executed this little work,
that, in consequence of sundry contradic-
tory reports and communications from
persons in America, unfriendly to revivals,

considerable doubts as to their character
have been entertained by Christians in
England; and that some persons who had
indulged respect for them at first, have
had that respect shaken. He is glad to
be able to say, that not a paragraph in
this volume has been written under such
an impression—although he has anticipated such results, as was reasonable. It
is impossible, in such a world as this, but
that ' the very elect will often be deceived,' on subjects and facts of the greatest importance, and of the most vital interest to the church—such is the power of
the enemy of all righteousness. It is only
those who have been in the midst of Revivals, that can appreciate their character
—and when Christians in England are
so well certified of the host of most venerable names, among the ministers of the
United States, who as fully believe, that
these revivals are the work of the Holy
Spirit, as that the Bible itself is—such a
fact ought to weigh strongly against a

few unfriendly reports, from a few more doubtful names. There is no good thing on earth, which has not been misrepresented—especially if it be of great public importance. And good men should always expect it.

The Author hopes it will be seen, from previous remarks, that this work is not a gratuitous office on his part—that it has been Providentially, and unexpectedly urged upon him. He has been assured, in the meantime, from sources which he has felt obliged to respect, that a collected and thorough view of American Revivals, if they are to be regarded as the work of God, is a great desideratum in England, and of vital consequence to the settlement of the public mind, as nothing but scraps has yet been before it. He would not, indeed, dare to claim such importance to this Essay, as to presume to hope that it will supply such a demand. Any extensive historical detail, it has not been in his power to give, as he never could have anticipated the necessity of being furnished with documents. And if he had foreseen it, such information is very much wanting even in the United States, in any collected, tangible form. His principal and grand aim, throughout this volume, has been—to define and establish the *character* of American Revivals. How far he has succeeded in that, remains for the Christian public in England to judge, so far as the work may claim and secure their attention. Although he professes to have done little in the *historical* part, he has presumed to promise something on that head in the title-page— for which, if there should be any disappointment, he hopes to be excused—and that it will be generously allowed, he has said enough to justify the title.

The Author has often been aware, in the progress of the work, that he might in some instances seem to be using bold language for a stranger, and that some might imagine he was exceeding the bounds of that diffidence and modesty, which become a foreigner. He hopes, however, it will not appear, that he has indulged largely in this way, on any topics of a local and delicate nature. And all reasonable persons will easily see, that no subject of general and great public interest, can be discussed with manliness and dignity, unless the public will award the privilege of speaking with great freedom. Every man is indeed bound to be circumspect and prudent, in whatever he undertakes, in which his fellow-creatures are interested with himself. And when he has conscientiously tried to be so, if in any respect he is thought to have failed, a generous allowance is all he can claim, and what he may reasonably hope to receive. The Author has wished to claim the privilege of a Christian speaking to Christians, on a subject of great public interest to the Church throughout the world—embracing a series of notable dispensations of Providence, asserted and believed to be the work of the Holy

Spirit. And nothing, but positive immorality, would be to him a subject of deeper regret, than to have exhibited the appearance of assuming the office of instruction, or a spirit of dictation. And if in any instance he shall seem to have been too confident, he prays it may be put to the account of that charity, which every Christian owes to a Christian brother. Let it be regarded as an error of judgment, or an excess of zeal, or anything, but a willingness to offend against propriety.

It will be seen by those, who have heard the Author's public discourses upon this subject, that he has here abandoned the train of thought pursued on these occasions, and selected sundry grand topics, the discussion of which would naturally cover the whole ground, and tend more directly and comprehensively to present what has been his constant aim—the proper *character* of these dispensations.

It may be said, perhaps, that the Author has brought in some great questions, which do not necessarily belong to the subject. Of that, however, he can only say—that in his own judgment, they have seemed to have an important relation.

He has been studious to avoid, as much as possible, all questions involving theological controversy—and yet, it was very difficult not to make some approximations occasionally to topics, respecting which there are always some speculative differences of opinion. If in any instances he may seem to be severe, it will be a source of regret. One can hardly be in earnest, without sometimes using strong language.

This trifling contribution to the religious literature of the day, forced upon the Author unexpectedly and reluctantly, he now commends to the candour of British Christians, and to the governance of the Head of the Church, praying and hoping, that if it shall do no good, it may do no harm.

CALVIN COLTON.

London, March 1, 1832.

AMERICAN
REVIVALS OF RELIGION.

CHAPTER I.

DEFINITION.

CHRISTIANS in England are sufficiently certified, that there have been, and still are occurring, in the United States of America, great public religious excitements, powerfully affecting the public mind in the regions thus visited for the time being, by affecting the minds of numerous individuals;—the result of which ordinarily is the apparent and hopeful conversion of many souls unto God, by tens, by fifties, and by hundreds, according to the power of the visitation, and the extent of the communities thus affected. And these excitements, as is known, have received the current, and for aught that can be objected, the appropriate denomination of *Revivals of Religion*.

A revival, therefore, may be defined, as,—*the multiplied power of religion over a community of minds, when the Spirit of God awakens Christians to special faith and effort, and brings sinners to repentance.*

American revivals, I have thought, may properly be divided into two classes: one, when the instruments are not apparent; the other, when the instruments are obvious.

The former class have sometimes come ' like a sound from heaven, as of a rushing mighty wind,' overwhelming, almost instantaneously, the minds of a whole community with a deep, religious solemnity — filling the impenitent with alarm, and Christians with expectation. And yet the instruments of such a visitation would not be apparent. They have seemed to come directly from the presence of the Lord, unasked for, unexpected. What secret, unknown intercourse may have been had with God, on such an errand, by some of the most humble and secluded of his children, yet ' full of faith and of the Holy Ghost ;'—what prayers of intercessors, long in heaven, have been remembered and answered by these visitations ;—what covenant mercies, having respect to fathers, who for generations have been asleep in the grave, these may be descending upon their children ;—or how much of it may be owing to that sovereign kindness of God, which goes beyond his covenant—which disappoints expectation by bestowing more than has been asked, by opening the windows of heaven, and pouring out a blessing larger than the measures prepared to receive it ;—which, or what parts of all these considerations may have moved the mind of God to such signal displays of his grace —or which principally, it is impossible to say. This question will probably remain a secret, till the day of final revelation.

At other times, revivals of this same class— (the same, so far as the invisibility of instruments is concerned) have come, ' like a still, small voice,' stealing softly and unseen over the minds of numerous individuals, apparently in insulated circumstances relating to each other, spreading deeper and wider, until some season of public religious assembly would furnish a natural occasion for the commingling of sympathy, and the unexpected development of a common and irrepressible feeling—so that all would feel, that God was in the midst of them by the special power of his Spirit. And yet, neither in this would the particular instrumentality be obvious.

In this first class of revivals, the hand of God has always been more undeniable. For nobody expected, nobody prayed, nobody tried for such a work—so far as appeared. And this, till a few years past, was the more ordinary character of revivals of religion in America : churches and Christians waited for them, as men are wont to wait for showers of rain, without ever imagining, that any duty was incumbent on them, as instruments. And it is only within a few years, that the promotion of revivals by human instrumentality has, to any considerable extent, been made a subject of study, and an object of systematic effort.

And hence the *second* class of revivals—or what I have chosen to distinguish as such, for the sake of marking the historical progress and the changing character of those events in the United States, passing under this general denomination. The first class of revivals I regard as a school of Divine Providence, in which God was training the American church for action—and raising up a corps of disciplined men, gradually augmenting in number, who should begin to see and feel— more practically—that, although, in every work of grace, ' the excellency of the power be of

God,' yet men are ordained to be the *instruments* of converting and saving souls—and the instruments of Revivals of Religion.

Although I would not presume to attach an equal relative importance of the first class of revivals to the second, as the age of miracles held to the ordinary succession of the Christian dispensation — yet there has seemed to me a likeness in the two histories;—in so far, as when the purposes of miracles were accomplished, they gave place to the succession of the ordinary influences of the spirit; so the first class of revivals, which I have named, having trained up a host of advocates, and graduated them, as it were, from pupilage to the office of leaders, has been gradually giving place to the second—instances of the former becoming more and more infrequent, and those of the latter more and more common.

That common apology for indolence, which clothes itself with the sanctity of a resignation to the divine will—' *we must wait God's time* '— has been too often and too long employed in the United States, in application to the coming of Revivals of Religion. But it is now getting to be more generally understood, that to wait God's time, in this matter, is not to wait at all;—and that sitting still, or standing still, is not the submission of piety, but an expression of the sloth and recklessness of unbelief. Revivals of Religion now — at least to some extent — are not simply regarded, as things to be believed in, as possible with God, and then resigned to God, as though man had nothing to do with them; but they are laid out as fields of labour, in which it is expected man will be a co-worker with God. They are made matters of human calculation, by the arithmetic of faith in God's engagements.

But is not this second class of revivals more like the work of man than the first?—Yes; and there is actually more of the work of man in them—and not the less genuine for all that. In the *first* class, God works in spite of and against the want of human instrumentality;—he works against all the opposing tendencies of the prayerlessness, and the inactivity, and the very *counter*-workings of his people—and of his ministers even. ' He is found of them who seek him not, and who call not after him.' He works as a sovereign, executing, not more than he has decreed, but more than he has promised.

In the *second* class, also, he works as a sovereign ; because it is one part of his sovereignty, (a part too often overlooked,) to meet his own engagements, to fulfil his promises—to work when his people work, and to work with them. God often does more of good than he promises, but he never does less. In the former revivals, the visitations of God were more awful, because he seemed to come alone, and in all the mightiness of his power. Men stood still and wondered, as his conquering chariot rolled along. All heard the sound, and witnessed the thronging of the multitudes in the way. And the fruit of these visitations has been, that multitudes of perishing souls, as the Saviour passed by, have lifted up their voice, and cried, ' Jesus, thou Son of David, have mercy on us,' and have been heard, and forgiven, and sanctified.

But although God may work when his people are asleep, and disappoint all their expectations, by opening on their astonished eyes the wonderful works of his spirit, yet God never sleeps when his people work. And when they work in obedience to his will, he will own their labour, and add to it the work of his own hand. Such is the reasoning, and such the faith of the advocates and the systematic promoters of revivals of religion in the United States. They take God at his word—viz. ' That he has no pleasure in the *death* of the wicked, but that he should *turn* and *live*.' And they go and warn him in the name of the Lord, and he does turn. They consider it a matter settled by an unequivocal Revelation :—that the conversion of sinners and the salvation of souls is agreeable to the will of God—' as many as the Lord our God shall call,' by the voice of his servants, in their voluntary and benevolent enterprises, as well as by other means; and that, however the people of God might possibly mistake in some other enterprise, the warrant for which is not so clearly expressed, they can never mistake in this :—' Go out into the highways and hedges, and *compel* them to come in '—is the command. Compel *all* indiscriminately. It is not for you to make the selection.

I have intimated, that the more ordinary character of revivals of religion in the United States, *formerly*, was a visitation of the Spirit of the Lord upon a community, unexpected, and apparently unasked. God did not seem to wait for instrumentality in its common visible forms.

But *now,* the ordinary character of the same events is the divine blessing upon measures concerted and executed by man, where the instruments are obvious. A host of ardent, devoted revival men have been raised up in the school of former and later revivals, whose ranks are continually increasing, and who are becoming more and more experienced, and more and more successful. And every fresh revival, of any considerable extent, multiplies candidates for the ministry, who will never forget the day, nor the place, nor the circumstances, of their new birth; and who, after a suitable training and culture, themselves enter the field, and become active and efficient revival men. The spirit of revivals is born into them, and bred with them, and makes their character. And, so far as I know, the revivals which are now going over that country, are principally brought about by such instrumentality. The exceptions to this rule, I believe, are rare; and hence it may be expected, that they will continue and increase, till they shall have overspread the land; and may it not be hoped, till they shall have overspread the nations, and the world?

CHAPTER II.

IMAGINE a sinner awakened, and led on to conversion by reflection ; having, in the mean time, little or no intercourse with other minds on the subject of religion, but associating principally, or exclusively, with his Bible, and communing alone with his own heart, and with God. Scarcely a second person is aware of the state and progress of his mind, except, if he is concerned in the common intercourse of life, the more than usual gravity and seriousness of his demeanour will naturally be observed. There are, doubtless, a great many conversions of this sort ; and they may be called, in distinction from another class, *insulated* conversions.

Suppose an individual has been awakened by the admonitions of a sermon, or of some private intercourse with other minds, and is conducted by the spirit of God to the stage of genuine conversion, but is virtually alone in this state and progress of his mind, there being no second person in his neighbourhood, in a similar condition—this may also be called an insulated conversion, though not so absolutely so, as the other case supposed. There was, indeed, a social influence, which first awakened his attention; but no sympathy of other minds in a like condition, either to originate instrumentally, or to urge on his career. There is little reciprocal influence between such conversions and society.

We may suppose, again, a community of greater or less extent, bound together by many common ties of a social character, through the channels of which sympathy on all subjects of common interest, especially those calculated to agitate the mind, is easy and quick. It may, farther, be supposed, that the Spirit of God arrests the attention of an unconverted individual of such a community, producing a very anxious solicitude for the salvation of his soul—so anxious, that he cannot keep it a secret, if he would. It is, moreover, supposed, that this community are generally instructed in the doctrine of repentance, as essential to peace with God,—and of regeneration, to salvation. It is the common public opinion—the popular belief, by an habitual speculative assent. Of course it is an easy and natural step to the conclusion, that it is quite reasonable, and even important, for every individual, at some period of his life, to devote himself, in special earnest, to his own preparation for eternity—that he is in danger of being overtaken in his sins by death. When, therefore, an individual of such a community is suddenly and powerfully seized with a concern for his soul's eternal welfare—so powerfully that he cannot conceal it—that his feelings break out in tears and in prayers—that he throws himself upon the compassions of Christians, as more fitted to guide his anxious mind, and to be his intercessors with God—and that, of necessity, the matter becomes a subject of some public notoriety—it very naturally produces a pause in the ordinary career of those with whom this individual is more intimately allied. And it may also be supposed, that the same Spirit which has smitten the individual with a conviction of his guilt, and a sense of his danger, employs that very event, as an instrument of awakening his former associates to an equal degree of concern, so that they not only pause at his arrest, but are themselves arrested, finding that they too are involved in the same condemnation, and have need of the same pardoning mercy and sanctifying grace. And now a group of individuals are together, asking, with an affecting and overpowering earnestness—What must we do to be saved?

And this increase of the number renders it still more a matter of public notoriety; and there is a general pause. Every individual of this group has his more intimate connexions with society, as the first individual had with them; and for the same reasons, and we will suppose, by the same Divine influence, the number of the anxious is soon multiplied, till a crowd of individuals are together asking and seeking the way of salvation; and soon a whole community are affected, in a greater or less degree. All sympathise. Christians are ' filled with faith and the Holy Ghost,' and with an uncommon spirit of prayer; they are excited to diligence and roused to activity. The minister or ministers of religion are greatly animated, and uncommonly furnished by the natural excitements of such a state of things. The house of God is thronged, and the assemblies deeply affected and impressively solemn. Every sermon, and every prayer, and every exhortation, seem to tell with amazing power on the congregated multitudes. Sinners are converted, and others awakened, and the work goes on with increasing power, extending through the community. Meetings are necessarily multiplied, to meet the exigencies; ministers and Christians have as much as they can do to attend to the anxious, to guide the inquiring, and to conduct the frequent public assemblies of the people. They visit from house to house, warning the careless, encouraging and confirming the trembling hope, rejoicing with those who rejoice, instructing, exhorting, and offering up prayer. And this is somewhat the manner of an American revival of religion. And the fruit of it is, that many sinners are hopefully born again, the church enlarged, believers improved in their Christian character, the interests of religion obtain a wider and more solid foundation in the community, and the way is better prepared for another season of like refreshing influence from above.

And this is what may, perhaps, with propriety, be called the *relative* and *social* influence of religion, under the operation of the Spirit of God. It differs from *insulated* cases of conversion, before described, as combining the amazing and incalculable power of human sympathy, and through this medium multiplying itself, like the plenteous shower, which comes pouring down in immediate succession of the first few and scattered and herald drops. It is an admirable economy of God, in touching one heart by his Spirit, to prepare the way for touching many hearts,—to convert the social principles of our nature, from occasions of accumulated mischief and untold evil, to which they have been, and are, continually perverted, into instruments of a purifying and redeeming agency. Man is a social being. And it is no less true, that sin will multiply itself, through the medium of such a nature, with an untold rapidity and power, when once the channel is opened and polluted,—than that holiness, by the redeeming agency of God's Spirit, may march with equal strides, by the same principle, to the re-establishment of its own empire. Or perhaps it is more correct to say, that the social principle is made available by the Holy Spirit in the execution of his convincing and regenerating offices. And none but those, who have been in the heart of such scenes, can estimate its amazing power.

I am aware that this may be taken by some, as a confession of what has been by them supposed :—that American revivals owe their peculiarities to sympathy. What is true is not to be denied. A part of the secret, if there be any, no doubt lies here. But it is to be added : ' The excellency of the power is of God.' I know not, nor am I able to see, that the full admission of all that can be made of this, is any disparagement to these revivals. The social principle is, doubtless, the grand *medium*, and that is all. But it can never account for the power, or extent, or results of the work.

Insulated conversions, as I have defined them, are sparse, notwithstanding the mighty apparatus of means, with which Christianity is furnished, and in the bosom of which they occur. And those means, in such cases, are actually sluggish in their operation, and seem greatly embarrassed in accomplishing the result. I speak of fact. But when the social principle comes in as a medium and minister of Divine truth, ' the word is quick and powerful, sharper than two-edged sword.' The sympathies of our nature catch the hallowing fires of the Spirit, or rather, the Spirit seizes upon them, and runs from heart to heart by the common laws of social influence, and multiplies the subjects of his purifying grace, in proportion as the ties of a community are intimate, and dispose them to sympathy—apparently so. Insulated conversions are comparatively sullen, and cold, and cheerless. The grand talisman of the social state lies dormant ; the holy fire is not felt by others, because they are not near enough to feel it. That God could produce a revival of religion, independent of this principle, is not for us to affirm, or deny. He can doubtless multiply cases of conversion without it, to an unlimited extent ; but he is not accustomed to group such cases. The moment they are grouped, the social principle operates, and the isolated condition is merged in a community of feeling And according to the definition I have given of a revival, it implies the operation of this principle.

It is generally understood, that the state of society in the United States is very near to a common level. And so far as the sympathies of community are concerned, on any subject of great and common interest, it is agreeable to fact. Especially is it so in those regions, where revivals of religion originated, and have principally flourished. It may be said of all the minor communities, of which the grand community is composed, that, in each of them, every body knows every body, and feels an interest in every body ; so much so, that nothing of material interest transpires with a family, or scarcely with an individual, but that a pulse of sympathy beats through the whole body. From the first settlements of New England, the incorporated townships and parishes have had a common centre, where, on the Christian Sabbath, they meet together on common ground, are mutually recognised, instructed by their spiritual pastors in the cardinal and practical doctrines of religion,—among which the office of the Holy Spirit, and the necessity of regeneration, have been habitually and especially laboured and enforced. The child, who did not understand these doctrines, must have been very stupid.

Such being the state of society, and religion being generally acknowledged and esteemed the paramount interest of man, and withal, the public conscience being preserved pure and susceptible, it is not very difficult to see, that the marked conversion of one or more individuals might become a subject of common and public interest. And admitting the scripture doctrine of the office and special agency of the Holy Spirit in the work of conversion, the change might well be regarded with a high degree of respect and reverence. It has ever been considered as a great and decided change—a change which every one must undergo, in order to salvation. It has been habitually urged and pressed upon the conscience, as a present duty. With a public mind so enlightened, and a conscience so susceptible, and a common sympathy so all-pervading, it can hardly appear incredible, that the awakening of one sinner should be the means of awakening others, and the conversion of one the means of other conversions. Especially if we believe in the proper office of the Holy Spirit,— in the promise and purpose of God as revealed, and in the power of the social principle. And more especially still, if we consider that the common belief favoured and anticipated such results, as the genuine fruit of the Spirit.

CHAPTER IV.

**THE REASONABLENESS OF REVIVALS, AS EVENTS
TO BE EXPECTED, EQUALLY AND JOINTLY FROM
THE NECESSITIES OF THE GRAND DESIGN OF
CHRISTIANITY, FROM THE CHARACTER OF MAN,
AND FROM THE DIVINE AGENCY REQUIRED AND
EMPLOYED TO REFORM THE WORLD.**

EVERY one knows, or may know, that the design
of Christianity is to bring back this apostate
world to God—to reduce the kingdoms and the
men of this world to the reign of Messiah—
to recover mankind from a state of rebellion
against their Maker, to the submissions of obedience—and to make the subjects of this grace
holy on earth, and eternally happy in heaven.
It is to *reduce* the world, and the whole world,
by a system of moral means and agencies. This
is certainly a stupendous scheme, a sublime enterprise, characteristic and worthy of that Almighty Being, who has devised and undertaken
it. It alike dazzles by its glories, and con-
founds by its apparent impracticabilities. But
there is nothing too mighty for God.

peculiarity, and its deep and thrilling power. And it is equally evident, that there is something more than human sympathy—that human sympathy could never induce such results. This attribute of our nature is a *medium*, in such case, but not an efficient cause—it is the medium of Divine influence. The Spirit of God, taking hold of it, as an instrument, facilitates, and (if I may be allowed the expression) economises his own powers. He avails himself of channels already open, as the currents of his own influence. Instead of confining his powers to subjects in insulated conditions, as in the case of sinners standing alone, unconnected with society, he touches a pulse, which beats in many hearts, —he touches a heart, in which a thousand others are interested by mediate connexions.

It is not because the Holy Spirit has need of such facilities, and yet it is a facility, even to God, if I may say so. It is an admirable economy. It is putting in requisition for the best objects and for the most important purposes—for the renovation of human hearts and of human society —that very principle, which thrills all heaven simultaneously with the same sentiment of holy rapture and exultation—and which makes a communion of horrors among the spirits of the damned :—It is the social principle.

It will be obvious, there is nothing in this principle to account for a great and sudden movement of a whole community, upon a subject, which, like that of the Christian religion, has been before them from time immemorial, with all its sanctions and with all its motives—nothing in it, independent of the coming in of a special influence—an influence which does not lie in the letter of Christianity. A community may be surprised by what is new—but everything in the letter of Christianity is old. A community may be greatly moved, by what naturally and deeply affects their passions, when unexpectedly brought before them, by the eloquence of the tongue, or under the affecting power of circumstances. All such excitements, however, can only be momentary. But that the histories, and doctrines, and truths of religion, in which the public mind had been thoroughly versed from the cradle, should suddenly be armed with an unwonted power, not only over the minds of individuals, but so as manifestly to affect a whole community, and operate a thorough change in the hearts and lives of many individuals of that community—is a fact, which, so far as I know, lies within the compass of no philosophy to account for, but that of the religion which is the instrument of the change, and which professes to solve the problem by a reference to the powers of the Holy Ghost. What reason is there, that one community should feel more than another, or one person more than another;—their education being the same, and other things equal, which belong to the same relations and influences of society? And what reason, that the same communities and the same persons should feel more at one time than another, under the same system of means? Independent of the Spirit of God, there is a mystery in this;—but with it, there is no mystery.

But I undertook to show, that the sympathetic economy of revivals is consistent with the operations of the Spirit of God. And yet the drift of my argument seems to have been—that revivals could not take place without the Spirit. And it is quite immaterial which of these propositions is established—as the latter involves the former—and the proof of the latter more than proves the former, not that it proves too much, but strengthens the position.

I have called that state of the public mind,

indicated by the term revival, *a sympathetic economy*, because it comprehends and expresses the thing, better than any other brief form of language I can at present devise. It indicates an excited and powerful action of the public mind, on the subject of religion, by the special agencies of God's Spirit, *through the medium* of the reciprocal influences of mind on mind. It is *sympathetic*, as between man and man, and as between God and man. The Spirit of God merges the minds of individuals especially, and the mind of a community generally, into a peculiar atmosphere of his own creation. And it is a special *economy*, or dispensation out of the usual course,—out of the usual course, I mean, as to past and general history. It is hoped, however, that it will not always be recognised as extraordinary. I insist, it is worthy of the name of a dispensation—and properly of a special economy—*relatively* so; and in regard to the common course of things in the moral world. And, moreover, that it is truly worthy of God, as its author. There is no philosophy, but the doctrine of the Holy Ghost, as revealed in the Bible, that can account for it.

I admit, indeed, that there may be, and have

been great public religious excitements, which, by the bad management of men, have produced very little good fruit. And I should hardly dare to deny, even in such cases, the presence and power of the Holy Spirit, as demonstrated in some examples, and to some extent. The work of the Spirit may be limited, and obscured, and exposed to reproach, by the vicious handling of unskilled, or unholy instruments. And this is a lamentable device of the adversary to bring the work of the Spirit into discredit—to excite disgust and apprehension, in relation to all public religious excitements. But still there is only one way by which the world can be radically reformed—and that is, by an earnest and energetic challenge made upon its errors—and that challenge, to be effectual, must be accompanied by the power of God—and these influences together must necessarily produce excitement—and there can be no excitement without danger of the perversion of excited powers. The remedial powers must be proportionally energetic, as the evil is stubborn; and men, society, the world, must be *schooled* to reformation. That system of Divine Providence, devised for the redemption of the world, is itself a school for man; and

man needs not only to be educated in its principles, but he must be trained to its discipline, by a course of severe, arduous, and more or less, in its incipient stages, *unfortunate* experiment, until he shall have learned to avoid the evil in the attainment of the good.

But I wish not to be discursive—although there are constant temptations. My object, in this Chapter, has been generally to assert and to demonstrate the *consistency* of the sympathetic economy of a revival, with the operations of the Spirit of God. I have wished also to convey a just idea of what I mean by this sympathetic economy, as distinguished in its operations and results from what I have elsewhere denominated *insulated* conversions. The ordinary advance of the Church, in these days, is, by the latter class of conversions, good enough, and perhaps more apt to be genuine, in proportion to their nominal amount, but still not so decided and energetic in their character. And besides, they leave the world comparatively undisturbed in their spiritual slumbers, and the Church itself. But a revival challenges universal attention, and excites universal sympathy, in the regions thus visited; it burnishes and invigorates Christian

faith, excites to Christian enterprise, brings the unbelieving world to the pause of solemn reflection, and many sinners, often multitudes, are awakened and converted. Every body feels its influence.

I am disposed to believe, that the relatively increased power of the Holy Spirit in revivals of religion, will be sufficiently manifest from the nature of the work, as it stands connected with a multitude of minds, allied to each other by a sympathetic influence. None but those who have witnessed its operations can adequately conceive of its overwhelming character. It is the power of the Almighty Spirit, rousing at once an associated mass of human minds to reflection on the stupendous themes of religion, opening their eyes simultaneously to a discovery and sense of their alarming condition, as sinners unreconciled to God, conducting them to repentance and faith, and inspiring their hearts with sentiments, and filling their mouths with songs of praise.

CHAPTER III.

THE SYMPATHETIC ECONOMY OF REVIVALS CONSISTENT WITH THE OPERATIONS OF THE SPIRIT, AND GREATLY ENHANCING THE POWER OF THE SPIRIT RELATIVELY.

IF the reader be supposed to pass from the last chapter to this in order, he will probably understand what I mean by the phrase—*sympathetic economy of revivals.* I call it an *economy*, because it is strictly and distinctively so—and it is an economy of a wonderful character, and of wonderful power; and what makes it wonderful in both these respects, is, that the Spirit of God employs the social principles of our nature, as instruments in the mediate steps towards conversion—as the instruments of awakening attention and of conviction—so that when one mind is interested, another is interested—when one mind is deeply and powerfully exercised, another sympathises—when one is converted, another follows in train—and a third—and so on to a multitude. Human sympathy evidently has to do with it. And this is what constitutes its

The apparatus of this mighty scheme is all made ready—it was completed just 1800 * years ago. And why is not the work before this time achieved? If it may be supposed, that God makes the reasons of his own dispensations in any case apparent to man, by the developments of his providence for practical suggestion; and, if I may be indulged in conjecture, (call it only conjecture), without being accused of presumption, I would venture to specify, as one particular, in the solution of the question just propounded :—that the state of human society has never yet been ready.

Energetic and almighty as is the power of God's Spirit, the measure of his effectual grace, so far as appears, is, nevertheless, graduated by the states and conditions of society, and by the combination of the moral elements. And facts are no unimportant commentary for the ascertainment of true doctrine. Christianity is designed and calculated to subdue the world, but not without regard to means; not by physical miracles. It does not operate equally in unequal circumstances. ' Prepare ye the way

* Just 1800 years—one more or less—since our Saviour cried—' *It is finished.*'

of the Lord ' is equally applicable to every age, to every nation, to every community, and to every person. The way of the Lord *must* be *prepared.*

It is a fact, that 1800 years are gone, and the apparatus of Christianity is not yet brought into thorough operation. And there are, doubt-less, reasons for it—reasons nearer home, than in the heavens above, or in the depths beneath. Say not in thine heart, who shall go up to heaven to bring them down? Or who shall descend into the deep to bring them up? Be-hold, they are not there. The ' sin lieth at the door.' It may all be found in the unprepared-ness of man—of human society. Mankind have made shipwreck of Christianity. They have made it a convenience for their lusts; and by their perversions and abuses of its ordinances, they have retarded and kept in check its tri-umphs for nearly two thousand years. But in the mean time, God has been working favour-able changes. The utmost stretch of abuse, we may hope, has nearly worked itself out; and withal, Christianity has kept itself in the con-fidence of the world, and rather grown than diminished in its hold on the social fabric. God has been 'overturning and overturning,' until the great centres of political sway and social influence upon the earth are ready to shake off the abuse of power with the abuse of religion. And when this crisis shall have come, we may hope that the ' redemption of the world draweth nigh.'

One grand theatre, remote from the common turmoil of the nations, has already been prepared and opened for a fresh and interesting experiment of Christianity, and scenes of bright and hopeful omen have been enacting there for many generations. Where, it may be asked, has a state of society occurred, in the providence of God, since the opening of the Christian era, so favourable to the progress and triumphs of true religion, as in the United States of America? And where have the institutions and ordinances of Christianity been so signally blessed?

But it will, perhaps, be thought that I am running wide of the main proposition set at the head of this chapter. Rather so, I confess. But it has grown out of the question,—why is not the contemplated work of Christianity, for the reduction of the world, already achieved?—The apparatus, it was stated, is all ready; and it is evidently the declared purpose of God, that this apparatus shall at some period go into effectual and thorough operation—so that ' a nation shall be born in a day.' Admit that this language is figurative, there is enough in itself with its connexion, and in other parallel predictions, to justify the conclusion, that it is the design of God to institute, or rather to bring into operation a more energetic series of the dispensations of his grace, than the world has ever yet witnessed. Indeed, we may say, it is absolutely necessary, or else the hopes of the world, excited by Christianity, must be abandoned. But it is indisputable, that divine prophecy does unequivocally warrant expectations of the highest and most brilliant character—and that, too, in relation to the rapid march, and sudden triumphs of Christianity. As yet there has been nothing to satisfy this expectation. But arrangements for this purpose are doubtless in train, and it is pleasant to believe, if we can reasonably, that the symptoms of such a day are breaking upon us. It is interesting to observe the advancement of society in knowledge and in religion—in the ascertainment and confirmation

of the proper rights of man—and in the development of the symptoms of that approaching
crisis in society, from which the strides of progression shall outstrip the wings of faith, and
leave hope itself behind.

I will not suppose it necessary to prove, that
Christianity must advance, with a greatly, not
to say, immeasurably increased rapidity, beyond
all former example, in order not only to the fulfilment of its own inspired records—but equally,
to gain on the tendencies and force of human
depravity, to counteract its influences. In
what particular form, or forms, and at what particular period, these more rapid strides are to
be made, remains of course to be developed by
Providence,—except we are certified, it is to be
by the power of truth, through the efficacious
grace of the Holy Spirit; in other words, by the
moral suasion, combined in the entire apparatus
of Christianity. I do not say that American revivals are indubitably the signs of this approaching better day; nor that these are the exact
forms of the more rapid advances of Christianity
reasonably to be expected. But I do say, and
I shall endeavour in another place to prove, that
there are some striking and hopeful peculiarities

in these dispensations, worthy of the high respect and grave consideration of the Christian world; and that, if these are not, indeed, the work of God, and in a form very hopeful for the world, the date of the triumphs of Christianity must be put farther forward than I am willing to allow. For myself, ¡I cannot be satisfied that the world can ever be reduced, as Christianity contemplates, by what I have denominated *insulated* conversions. Under such dispensations, as it seems to me, irreligion, or the common worldly mass of unbelief, must for ever hold the vantage-ground. Society, the world, must be melted down in a common crucible, or else the moral elements will still remain heterogeneous, dissociate, and discordant. In theory, a genuine revival, as I would define it, is exactly and in all respects calculated for the universal amalgamation and purification of society. I am aware, that theory, unreduced, is little worth. But, in this instance, it is the fact which gives being to the theory, and which supports it: and I do humbly and honestly conceive, that events of this sort were reasonably to be expected, equally and jointly, from the necessities of the grand design of Christianity, and from the character of man.

In other words, the character of man, all the world over, cannot be thoroughly reduced in submission to Christ—Christianity cannot verify its own predictions,—independent of the introduction and support of a series of dispensations, of a character analogous to those of revivals of religion.

And yet more than all are such events, as revivals of religion, to be expected, in some such form as I have defined, from the introduction and employment of such a special and foreign agency as that of the Holy Ghost; that being necessary for the effectual reduction of human hearts and of human society. If common social influences, inherent in man, had been adequate for the religious reformation of the world, by the use of the motives presented in the simple letter of the Bible, without any superadded agency from above, and if such had been the purpose and the economy of God,—no such events as revivals of religion need have been expected—no such events could have occurred. But when it is equally a doctrine of fact, as of revelation, that the human heart is too stout and too determined in sin to surrender to the common influence of mind over mind, even when that influence comes armed with all the motives and sanctions of religion; when, indeed, this common social influence, combined as it is with human depravity, and left to itself, only rivets the chains of sin with greater power upon the human heart; when it is found absolutely indispensable for an Almighty agency from above to come in, and by a moral force to arrest attention, break the heart, and purify and convert the currents of its affections and passions; on these suppositions, accordant alike with facts, and the doctrines of religion, it were rational to expect a shock of human passion in the conversion of a sinner. And when it is understood, that for the rapid multiplication of conversions, God will pour out his spirit upon the people in mass, the very nature of man, as well as the overwhelming character of this influence, coming from a foreign source—from above—might lead us to expect a general and public convulsion of feeling. I say, *overwhelming*, for after all, and in all cases, the work of the Spirit in conversion is of this character. And that not to destroy, or even qualify the freedom of moral agency. It is merely making a depraved and perverse will *willing* to do right; not by the enforcements of a physical, but by a moral influence. And when this Almighty agency comes down upon a community to *multiply* converts, availing itself of the sympathetic powers of our nature to arrest general attention to the great and common concern—it were reasonable to expect a general and extraordinary commotion of feeling—it were stupid not to expect it. It were impossible it should be otherwise.

———

CHAPTER V.

THE CONNEXION OF AMERICAN REVIVALS WITH THE SPIRIT OF THE PILGRIM FATHERS.

' I am the God of Abraham, and the God of Isaac, and the God of Jacob.' ' I am the God that keepeth covenant.' And this is enough— enough to account for any, and ever so many blessings on the descendants of those men, who for conscience sake were driven out from these regions of the old world, and compelled to take refuge, and make a home for themselves and their children, on the distant shores of the new. He who is inquiring after moral causes must look higher than the philosophy of paganism—he must come up to the philosophy of Christianity. And he who is bestowing his thoughts on that experiment of human society, which has been in progress in North America for two centuries past, would run wide of truth in his conclusions of the influences operating there, if he did not take into his account the more than human agencies which Christianity brings in aid of its faithful adherents. The Pilgrims * are not to be judged by common rules; they were above the common order, as if born and trained for more than common purposes—which, indeed, was the fact. God raised them up for the special exigency, which they occupied and filled out, *viz.*, to lay the foundations of a new social edifice, to assort and throw into form the elements of a new empire. And the religious care and faith with which they undertook and carried on, and achieved their work, have been alike a subject of ridicule among the profane, and of approving admiration among those, who knew how to appreciate their character. And they did actually erect, not only a civil, but a religious empire—guarantying equally the rights of man in relation to man, and the duties of conscience in the relations of man to God. The spirit of religion was infused throughout, pervaded, and characterised all their institutions. Not that religion was imposed—but tolerated, patronised, recommended, exemplified — made

---

* A name, by emphasis, given by their descendants in New England to recognise, in a word, the injuries which drove them out from their homes, the character which they demonstrated, the enterprise which they undertook, and the achievements which they attained.

the chief ingredient of the moral structure—the leaven of the mass—welcomed cordially, cultivated assiduously.

By consequence, that structure of society, framed by these men, having retained its original stamp and the same grand features,—the same constitutional elements exercising a controlling power,—has always proved favourable to the operation of religious influence. There has always been a religious pulse in the community, that could be found, and easily susceptible of being quickened by the application of the proper means. And that pulse has extended through every limb to every finger's end. And to this day there are no barriers of *caste* in the United States —no impaled, insulated conditions of society, of a character to limit the common circulation of good and healthful moral influences—or to prevent a reformation, begun in one place, from reaching every other place. The messenger of God, who bears his commission to the heart and conscience of the most secluded individual in the land, may carry it also with equal boldness, if not with equal success, to the most exalted personage. No man can conveniently insulate himself from the approach of those influences, which pervade a body that is one, and of which he is a member.

It is more especially of society in New England that I make these remarks,—although they are more or less applicable to the whole community of the United States. And the origin of such a state of things is more especially to be traced to that spirit, which planted the colony of Plymouth. It was a sublime spirit of truly Christian enterprise. It is remarkable, that revivals of religion, under their American character, commenced in New England, and were, till quite recently, principally confined to that region. And their extension westward and southward, I believe, has generally been found in the track of New England emigrants, or springing up under the labours of New England ministers— until they are now beginning to be reported from every part of the land. The great bulk of revivals, however, are still found in the east and north. Such facts may be presumed to have a connexion with the original elements and peculiar frame of society, as also with the blessing of God in reward of the distinguished Christian virtues of the founders of such institutions, and of the fidelity of successive generations, in supporting them in their original spirit. It is a general and an exact truth—that the Pilgrim Fathers of New England laid the foundations of their civil and social edifice, and of their religious institutions, in tears, and prayers, and in much faith. And the experiment of two hundred years has proved, that God has regarded those tears, and remembered those prayers, and plenteously rewarded those works of faith.

From time to time, beginning in the earlier periods of the seventeenth century, down through successive generations, God has opened the windows of heaven, and shed down upon those regions the precious and large effusions of his Holy Spirit, as if to keep up an uninterrupted generation, and increase the host of witnesses for the truth. And what arrogance in supposing that such was the Divine purpose, and such its fulfilment? Indeed, when I have looked at the flight of the Puritans—as they have been ignominiously termed—or of our Pilgrim Fathers, as we have reverently called them—from these shores, to that far-off, uninviting, inhospitable continent, as then it was—I have, at the same time, been reminded of the woman in the

Apocalypse, who, ' her child being caught up to God and his throne, herself fled into the wilderness, where she had a place prepared for her of God, that they should feed her there.' God has, indeed, ' brought a vine out of Egypt, and cast out the heathen, and planted it. He has prepared room before it, and caused it to take deep root. And lo! it has filled the land! The hills are covered with the shadow of it, and the boughs thereof are like the goodly cedars. She hath sent out her boughs unto the sea, and her branches unto the river!'

———

CHAPTER VI.

HISTORICAL PROGRESS OF AMERICAN REVIVALS: —FIRST APPEARANCE—DECLINE—RE-APPEARANCE—PRESENT STATE AND PROSPECTS.

FIRST APPEARANCE.

THE forms of society, as organized by the pilgrim fathers of New England, have already been recognised, as favourable to religious influence. And a minute observance of the earlier history of those settlements, downward, will show, that religion was continuously the public care, and always inculcated, as the grand concern of every individual. Indeed, the primitive communities of New England were strictly and properly religious societies, the members of which had emigrated for conscience sake, and who set up their new establishments with fasting and prayer, and in the fear of God. And religion was all along a prominent and principal feature of their moral history. All its observances were conscientiously maintained in public, in the family, and in the closet. By the original terms of association, the public authorities, civil and ecclesiastic, assumed (whether wisely or unwisely) a parental guardianship over the morals and religion of individuals—a guardianship rarely refused for ages. It was rebellion against this assumption, which occasioned the unfortunate rupture between the Rev. Jonathan Edwards, and the people of his charge at Northampton, and his subsequent dismission in 1750. The external sway of religion, therefore, was for a long time maintained very much by authority—a sort of patriarchal influence—as at this day in the settlements of the Moravian church—pure, paternal, and energetic. In the mean time there were multitudes, and a constant succession of insulated conversions, as I have before denominated them, in distinction from conversions in revivals. And thus for more than a century after the first landing of our fathers at Plymouth (1622), religion and the church were sustained by a great uniformity of course—instrumentally and virtually by the weight of character, the original impress, and the presiding genius of the primitive fathers of New England.

But the time would come, and did come, when the buoyant spirits of youth and the motives of vigorous and enlarged enterprise, which that

new world presented, exhibited strong tendencies
to break loose from the primitive and somewhat
constrained conditions of society. Those conditions, or rules, were in some respects too rigid
to be endured—an error on the safe side—but
yet an error. And here was opened a new dispensation—a new era—under which God came
in by his Spirit to save what all the precautions
of the fathers of New England could not have
saved. So we hope, although the experiment is
still in progress. In reward of the fidelity of
those eminent servants of God, in answer to
their prayers, in covenant remembrance—and
more than all, or all in coincidence—in fulfilment,
as we hope, of the designs of God in opening
and peopling that new world, a new and extraordinary influence has been introduced for the
renovation of human hearts and of human society
—new in its forms and characteristics. For
aught that can be proved, and in all probability,
that simple and pure state of society, planted in
such a remote, secure, wide, and opening theatre
of human enterprise, was the first condition
of the combination of the most appropriate moral
elements, for the most advantageous displays of
Divine grace—that has presented since the esta-

blishment of Christianity. Certain it is, that the Christian religion has there been attended with a power and an efficiency, which, for its energy, for its long continuance, and for its increase, under the same identical forms, has not been before observed since the days of the Apostles. It is now exactly a century since these extraordinary phenomena of the human mind, under the influence of religion, began to be exhibited in those regions. And the notable accounts of them, drawn by the graphic and faithful hand of President Edwards, and by others his contemporaries, demonstrate generally and particularly the same features, as have been manifested all along from that time to the present, in those religious excitements, which are emphatically called revivals of religion. Let any one, conversant with the revivals of the present time, read the history of them, as they occurred in the days of President Edwards, and as reduced by his hand;—and under the minute, lively, and glowing representations, made by that excellent man, of those interesting scenes,— he will find himself in the same atmosphere, a witness of the same occurrences, as himself has felt with his own heart, and seen with his own eyes. He could hardly believe that a century of time occupied the interval between them. A century has rolled away, since these remarkable occurrences have been asserting their claims on the attention of the Christian world. And the history of them, in the mean time, is in no small degree interesting—especially, as it stands connected with their present increase, and rapid spread, and unexampled power. For never have revivals of religion in the United States been so numerous, or so powerful,—and never have they exhibited such promise of extension and permanent influence, as at the present moment.

The first appearance of American revivals, under their peculiar features, was during the active ministry of the Rev. Jonathan Edwards, Northampton, Mass., afterwards President of Nassau Hall, Princeton, New Jersey. They do not appear to have attracted public attention especially, till 1733, about which time and nearly simultaneously, apparently through the instrumentality of the faithful labours of Mr. Edwards and other excellent ministers of New England, many towns on Connecticut river, in the provinces of New Hampshire, Massachusetts, and Connecticut, as also towns remote from the river, were visited by those extraordinary influences, which have since constituted the characteristic marks of revivals of religion. And these visitations were continued for years, extending over the principal settlements of New England —were realised in some measure in the province of New Jersey, and if I do not mistake, on Long Island. They circulated extensively, were powerful, and exceedingly interesting for a period of ten or twelve years. Indeed, the great revival of New England, as it has generally been called, may be regarded as occupying the greatest portion of the period between 1730 and 1750.

In the mean time, George Whitefield lighted down upon those regions, as an angel of God. And he was welcomed as an angel of God, while he delivered the messages of God to the many thousands, who constantly flocked in his train, and crowded around his pulpit. Whitefield was an eminent instrument in the hand of God of rousing and augmenting the religious sensibilities of that wide and growing community, and of giving an impulse to revivals of religion, which is not yet spent, and I trust never will be. He came at a time, when the way was prepared for

D

him, and he had nothing to do but to pour forth
the overwhelming torrents of his eloquence, and
a blessing attended him wherever he went, as is
sufficiently known.

DECLINE.

The simple fact, that a period called the great
revival of New England, is noted and become
memorable in the religious history of that portion
of the United States, indicates conclusively that
there was a subsequent decline. But there has
never been a total suspension of those influences.
That notable visitation of the Spirit kindled up
fires all over the land, which have never been
extinguished, and which in an uninterrupted
succession have been breaking out in one place
and another, and sometimes have been displayed
in a very imposing manner, and to a very hopeful extent.

So far as human instrumentality has to do
in sustaining and promoting revivals of religion
(and that it is employed for this purpose there
can be no doubt), the reasons of the decline now
under consideration, and of the extent of its
duration, are perhaps sufficiently apparent:—

There was no experience in the Church, adequate to the exigencies and demands of such a state of things. It was an order of Providence, a mode of Divine dispensation, hitherto unknown—at least so far as regards any experience of the communities thus visited. Churches, ministers, the world were literally taken by surprise. The novel and energetic character of the influence attracted universal attention. And it necessarily challenged an opinion of its origin and merits, co-extensive with the impression of its extraordinary nature. A public opinion was to be formed concerning it, and it must pass the ordeal of that opinion. Admitting that it was of God, as we have reason to believe—admitting that it was the design of God to introduce and sustain an uninterrupted series of such dispensations, and finally to make them prevalent and universal—it is evident, that, so far as they were extraordinary, they must undergo a thorough experiment in their operation on human society. And it is reasonable to suppose, from analogical considerations, that just in proportion to the greatness and importance of the experiment, would be the severity of the test and the extent of its duration.

Christianity itself has been under experiment before the world, and on human society, ever since the fall,—although by gradual and slowly-progressive developments, until its Canon of Revelations was completed by the ministry of the Apostles. And since that time, it has been acting with all its combined forces. Its beginning, after all its apparatus of means was complete, was energetic, and triumphant. But it was destined to decline, and for the greatest portion of 1800 years has been labouring under all the disadvantages of abuse by its professed friends, and of the contempt and opposition of its enemies. God, doubtless, might have shortened this experiment, though not probably without sustaining an uninterrupted series of physical miracles. And besides, the first promulgations of Christianity, under its matured and perfect forms, were in the hands of inspired men, whose discretion, in the discharge of their apostolic functions, was infallible. Whatever they did, they did well and right. And they set up Christianity. But notwithstanding all the advantages of such a beginning, we know what have been the consequences.

My object in alluding to the experiment of

Christianity, as a whole, on human society, and to the results of that experiment thus far, is to show the reasonableness of expecting, by analogy, a corresponding operation of so important a part of the agencies of Christianity, as the special outpourings of the Spirit in these latter days; and also to illustrate the actual history of revivals of religion in the United States. If Christianity, as a whole, was doomed to decline, after having been put in operation by the ministry of inspired apostles—and to a long protracted decline of many centuries—it is not marvellous, that the introduction of the economy of revivals, the instrumental conduct of which has necessarily been committed to the hands of uninspired and inexperienced men, should be succeeded by some of those results, which the imperfections of God's own people and the wickedness of his enemies have always brought in to embarrass and impede the plans of God's redeeming mercy.

The great revival of New England, in the days of Edwards, was a new scene—new to those among whom it occurred, and in many respects new to the world. It astonished men's minds. It excited many people, professing to act under its influence, so much, as in some instances to throw sound judgment from its balance, and expose them to indiscretions. Some even of the best men, being full of expectation, from the ardour of their spiritual affections, were prone to go beyond the bounds of prudence. As the gift of tongues, in the days of the Apostles, when once conferred, became the property of individuals, committed to their discretion, liable to abuse, and was actually abused in some instances to the purposes of mere ostentation ;—so were these remarkable effusions of the Holy Spirit, and the hitherto unknown excitements in individuals and in communities, which they produced, also liable to abuse, in the hands of imperfect, uninspired men—and to some extent were abused—abused by their professed friends, and perverted by their enemies. Neither churches nor ministers had any experience in the management of the public mind in such a state of things.

It is evident, unless God were to support a series of continuous miracles, that ministers and churches and the world must be *trained* to the dispensations of Divine grace, in their more remarkable forms, whenever they occur. And it is reasonable to suppose, that such training should occupy time, involve mistakes, and perhaps a long succession of evils, from the known fallibility and rashness of man. Indeed, a training of this kind upon the largest scale, as we have just noticed, has actually been going on, under the most grievous mistakes and catastrophes, for 1800 years. It is seen by this, that God could not bring in the redeeming ordinances and means of Christianity, without their being subjected to abuse and perversion for a long series of ages. But we hope the saddest calamities of this description have gone by. The Protestant reformation, great and good as it was, has been abused and fearfully perverted upon the very premises, where first the splendours of its light burst upon the world, and the energies of its doctrine sundered the chain of Papal oppression. And so also that more fresh and that brighter scene of the revival of primitive Christianity, which began to spread over the plains of New England, one hundred years ago, was, in some respects, marred and clouded by human imperfection. But the state of society there was, in the first place, too simple and too pure—and next too remote from the foreign incursions of vitiating influences, to suffer any considerable relapse. The very basis, on which the reformation by revivals was commenced, was made up of the purest elements of a previous reformation of Christianity—retaining, indeed, the common pravities of our nature, and for that reason destined to struggle with disadvantages.

RE-APPEARANCE—OR AS IT MIGHT MORE PROPERLY BE TERMED—REVIVAL OF REVIVALS.

It is not true, as already recognized, that revivals have totally ceased at any time, since their first appearance in our country. It is well known, that within forty years past, the Christian world in England and in the United States, have been greatly awakened to a benevolent regard for the heathen, and that within this period they have originated numerous grand enterprises in their behalf. The revival of this truly Christian and missionary spirit, as was very natural, has challenged and called into action, in the American churches, the kindred spirit of revival at home. The *feeling* existed before,—has never been entirely dormant for a century. Prayer and effort for the heathen have excited prayer and effort for those perishing at our own doors. The two sentiments have had a reciprocal action to invigorate each other. They have grown up in company to a maturity and manhood of character. They are always found in company—rarely apart. Just in proportion, as the spirit of domestic revival reigns, there reigns the spirit of foreign missionary enterprise. And as the latter is a sober, calculating, sublime spirit—a living principle, rather than a fitful flame—it imparts the same character to the former. Contemporaneously with the revival of the missionary spirit, in the United States, which for a generation past has been constantly rising and spreading, multiplying itself into itself, combining its forces and augmenting its power—has its kindred spirit risen, and prevailed, and waxed strong, and become 'mighty through God.' That is no longer the young and inexperienced principle of a day, which appeared in New England a century ago, in the cradle of its infancy. It has left that unripe age forever behind,—it has experienced the chilling repulses and rough encounters of a rude world,—it has been made familiar with disaster, and forced in a thousand forms to make acquaintance with the devices of the adversary. It is no longer a child, but it is armed with the wisdom and experience of manhood. All former disasters are so many beacons of advice, watched at every turn, or descried over every foaming surge. As remarked in a former chapter, revivals of religion in the United States have grown into a system of calculation, and the means of originating and promoting them are made equally a subject of study, as of prayer, and the ground of systematic effort. It is a grand and habitual subject of mutual counsel among Christians and Christian ministers, and has been for years, not only at ordinary public meetings, and at the common opportunities of intercourse — but there have been held great public conventions of those most experienced in revivals, collected from remote parts of the country, for the sole purpose of agitating and settling the great and fundamental principles of promoting revivals. The religious newspapers and periodicals have teemed with these discussions, in all their various forms. Not a sheet drops from these presses, but it has something to do with revivals. Among the most ardent and enterprising of Christians in the United

States, revivals are the great theme and constant aim, and they are becoming more and more so. It is a leading article of their creed, that the spirit of revivals is the efficient weapon and the great pioneer of Christian enterprise.

PRESENT STATE AND PROSPECTS OF AMERICAN REVIVALS.

And it has actually occurred, in the providence of God, that with the revival of this spirit, revivals of religion have been gradually multiplying, until they have become the grand absorbing theme and aim of the American religious world—of all that part of it, which can claim to participate in the more active spirit of the age.

As I have elsewhere remarked, the earlier revivals seem to have been a school of divine Providence, in which God was training his church and ministers for action, and raising up a corps of experienced and disciplined men—since which, revivals have exhibited a somewhat different character, in so far as the instrumentality of them has been more obvious. Scores of ministers, and hundreds of prominent, influential, and active Christians have been brought fully into this work, and put on the harness, not to take it off till death. And every fresh revival increases the number. Very many churches and their pastors are so thoroughly experienced in the work, by its frequent occurrence in their own congregations, as to be minutely acquainted with the various forms, under which the human mind and its affections are exhibited on these occasions, and demonstrate a skill in dealing with anxious and enquiring souls, as ready and apt, as the long practised physician of the body in prescribing for the patient under his hand. The atmosphere of a revival is not to them a strange and unwonted condition—but to be out of it is to be out of their element, and in a state of uneasiness and pain. And they will pray and labour without rest, until they again experience the refreshing visitation of the Divine Spirit.

American revivals have been so far redeemed from former disasters, from the reproach of bad management, and from the hands of inexperience, as to afford a rational ground of expectation, that from this hour an uninterrupted and increasing tide of triumph in this cause awaits that portion of the Church. It has been so fully demonstrated, and in so many instances, that a community can enjoy a revival of religion without extravagance, and without disturbing the ordinary movements and relations of society, so far as they are innocent and proper,—that opposition has greatly diminished, and common public opinion turned much in their favour. The people of the United States, more especially of New England, have been educated to a popular belief, that regeneration is essential to salvation; and the belief, or at least a tacit assent, is getting to be more and more the common impression, that revivals of religion are the most energetic and effectual means of multiplying cases of regeneration, and consequently are desirable.

It is seen and admitted by all, that those communities which have been most frequently visited with revivals, are in all respects the purest and the best,—that there are more Christians in them, and that Christians are more exemplary. These are known and observable facts; and facts of this description tell upon the public mind with invincible power. Men of high standing and influence have also been brought into the ranks of converts; and rarely does it happen, where the Church has been greatly increased by repeated outpourings of the Spirit, but that the greatest weight of character in the community is found at the Communion table.

The last fifteen years, in parts of the United States, especially in the east and north, have been an almost uninterrupted scene of extensive and powerful revivals, and generally of a grave and sober character, such as to command the respect of the world. And the period comprehended within a twelvemonth past, is unexampled in all previous history of the kind for the number and power of these remarkable visitations. They have taken faith itself by surprise, and overreached all expectation. And there is every indication at the present moment, from all the probabilities arising from moral causes in visible operation, that these revivals will go on, and still increase. The prospects of revivals now are not so dubious and uncertain as formerly. The instruments are more obvious. They have been brought into the field by the hand of man, and the continuous employment of them for the same purposes, is likely to be sustained with a multiplication of their number and power.

The present probabilities of the future uninterrupted increase and triumphant march of American revivals from this time, amount to a moral certainty. They have outlived and triumphed over disaster,—they have secured, in a very great measure, the favourable regards of the public mind, and are constantly gaining ground in this particular. They number in the ranks of their cordial friends and advocates a multitude of men, who in all respects are of the highest public consideration. The recent and present revivals have generally been brought about by a system of organized instrumentalities ; and those instrumentalities are constantly and rapidly augmenting in number, and power, and influence. And as they have hitherto invariably been owned and blessed of God, this success, it is considered, may reasonably be taken as a basis of calculation for the future. There is, of the two, a greater certainty of the success of moral, than of physical instrumentalities, when properly organized and applied—if it be proper to make such a distinction. The former never fail,— the latter may, and sometimes do fail. For instance :—a man may put seed corn in the earth, and be disappointed of a crop, for want of rain. But God has established a more intimate and more sure connexion between his blessing and the labours of Christian faith. The spiritual, or moral world is always susceptible of the influences by which it is visited.

———

CHAPTER VII.

By this time, in the progress of these discussions,
I hope the distinct and proper economy of a revival is sufficiently defined and well understood.
I have endeavoured to present it as a dispensation
of Providence, of a marked and peculiar character, brought upon a community by the outpourings of the Spirit of God, in fulfilment of the
predictions, and in execution of the design of
Christianity, for the more powerful, richer, and
more manifest displays of Divine grace, in the
greater and comparatively sudden increase of the
Church, by the conversion of many sinners in
company, augmenting the faith of Christians,
and invigorating their Christian character. It
is a special season, and to the Church a refreshing visitation. It is, as I have frequently
remarked, an economy of a distinct and peculiar
character, all the specialty of which is owing
entirely to the Spirit of God. As it is impossible

fully to appreciate the power of it, except by being immersed in its own atmosphere, and then only for the time being, so is it difficult to describe it by an ordinary technical definition.

I have elsewhere recognised the occurrence of revivals, the instrumentality of which has not been obvious. Of such facts there have formerly been many instances in the United States. And I cannot doubt it is one of the features of these dispensations of mercy to man, in the outset of a series in store for a nation or people where experience is wanting, that God pours forth his Spirit, like unexpected showers upon the thirsty earth. But although this may be a fact, and one part of the character of religious revivals, yet it is no less true, that obvious instrumentalities are employed, and that honest and earnest endeavours, skilfully applied, will be blessed for the attainment of this end. God may seem to work without his people, but he never refuses to work with them. And while we are bound to recognise and be grateful for unexpected visitations of this description, it is the instrumental and visible agencies of such events, as belonging to man, which concern us especially to study, and with which more especially we have to do. The Spirit of God is beyond our control; but our own voluntary powers, the right use of which he claims, and has promised to honour, are not so. I assume it then, that however God may be pleased, in his own gracious sovereignty, to originate revivals of religion, independent of visible human instrumentality, it is equally and invariably a part of his sovereignty to honour such instrumentality, in the accomplishment of the same result, when faithfully employed. And here is the province of our duty. And it is to this field of observation I would now direct the attention of my readers, for the specification of some of the *means* of originating and promoting revivals of religion, and some of the hinderances.

I say of *originating*, as every revival must have a beginning, and as I have reason to believe, means or instruments are equally appropriate in this office, as in promoting revivals after they are begun.

I will, in the first place, suppose a community to consist of a common and very desirable organization, with a sound Church and good pastor planted in the midst of them—sound and good in the common acceptation of these terms in such application. This community is supposed to consist of believers and unbelievers, (this distinction being intended simply to recognise the former class as professing Christians, without denying a speculative belief in Christianity to the latter), who as families and individuals are associated under a Christian ministry, for the maintenance of Christian ordinances. We will suppose this community in some degree insulated, like a country, or village parish, or congregation. For there is, doubtless, a difference between a city and a country congregation, in the existence and amount of a distinct community of feeling. We will allow, in this case, that the great and fundamental doctrines of Christianity are declared habitually from the pulpit, maintained by the Church, and not opposed especially by the people. But though the people attend regularly on the public means of grace, the interest they manifest towards religion is merely the respect of a decent civility. The Church, perhaps, are orderly, but not liable to the accusation of zeal. And, ' like people, like priest.' All are decent, and all asleep. The maintenance of civil order is the best that can be said of them. An insulated conversion may now and then occur, and the subject of it be brought into the Church. The question is:—what are the most hopeful means of bringing about a revival of religion in such a community?

I answer:—The minister of religion, as he is the appointed administrator of the word and ordinances of Christianity, the acknowledged public guardian and advocate of the cause of his master, should be first and principal, in challenging the cordial and unqualified submission of the people of his charge to the message, which he is commissioned to deliver. And he must do it too, with an earnestness so real, that his people cannot be left in doubt, whether he be in earnest; ' commending himself to the conscience of every man.'

> ' By him the violated law should speak
>   Its thunders—and by him, in strains as sweet
>   As angels use, the Gospel whisper peace.
>   Much impressed
>   Himself, as conscious of his awful charge,
>   And anxious mainly, that the flock he feeds
>   Should feel it too.'

And in order to this he must be a man of faith, and a man of prayer. He must be ' full of faith and of the Holy Ghost.' He must believe that sinners *can* be converted—and feel that they *must* be converted. And, not forgetting, that the Holy Spirit has to do with this work, as well as human instrumentality—that the Holy Spirit is the efficient power—his first applications should always and habitually be, at the throne of grace. When he goes out to his work, he should get his spirit and put on his armour there. And when he returns he should fall down there, and commend his labour to God's blessing—he should plead, importune with God, and refuse to let him go without a blessing.

But what are some of the parts of his duty, when possessed of the proper spirit? He has a Church; and he must seek to infuse a proper spirit into them. He must inlist their power, their influence, their intercessions with God. He must call them to fasting and prayer. He must persuade them to action. There is no impossibility in this, if they are Christians. They will recognise his spirit—they will feel the force of his appeals—they will follow him as a leader. And so many of them as will not respond to his appeals, and come up to his help, he must treat with all prudence in the sight of God, being careful not to make such a quarrel with them, as to disappoint his main designs. In this he must be meek, and then they cannot be in his way.

Himself and Church full of faith and prayer, (all of them that have any faith at all)—' having one mind and one spirit,' let him present himself before his people, the unconverted of his congregation, in all the earnestness, and with all the fervor and holy importunity of such a spirit, and as God is true, as his promises are valid and worthy of trust, as the Holy Ghost is Almighty, it can hardly be possible that his preaching and prayers will not be felt.

And such a spirit will be an excellent guide, for the selection of his topics for the pulpit, and for his manner of treating and applying them. There is nothing more true than that a minister may preach orthodoxy all his life, and do little good. His people's heads may be well stored with orthodoxy, and yet their hearts ' full of every unclean and hateful lust.' For a minister to be anxious mainly that his people should think right, having never learned that the best way to this is to make them feel right, is a real misfortune. The most effectual lodgment of truth in the mind, is when it has found its way there by the heart; and it is possible that a regenerated sinner should learn more of correct and practical theology in one day after his conversion, than he had ever attained in all his life, under the best tuition. What, indeed, can be more preposterous, as a principal aim, than the object of making orthodox theologians of an unconverted congregation? And what is gained, if they die in their sins, but a deeper hell? It is like a physician, lecturing on physiology, or materia medica, over his suffering and dying patient, instead of administering to his relief. I would not be thought to undervalue catechetical instruction and doctrinal training. I set a high value upon both. But it is a sad sight to see a congregation of impenitent sinners, imagining they are going to heaven, because they have got their Catechism in their pockets, and in their heads, when they are actually going down to hell. Give the Catechism and the Creed, but withal see that their pages be not left to the winds of heaven—that the seed sown be not snatched away by the Evil One.

A minister of the right spirit, resolved on the conversion and salvation of his hearers, as the object most important, and a duty most incumbent, will seek to lodge the most practical and pungent truths of revelation, deep in the affections of their souls. He will find out and follow up the avenues to the heart. It will be a constant aim with him to stir up Christians, and to awaken sinners. That minister has made a high attainment in the economy of his profession, who has discovered, that the best way to edify believers, is, to set them to pray for the conversion of sinners;—and to give them an opportunity of witnessing the conversion of sinners in answer to their prayers. There is nothing gives such a spring to true piety, as such employment, and such results;—nothing so much purifies and invigorates it;—nothing makes it so buoyant, or gives it such an onward impulse in its march towards heaven;— nothing so well qualifies the mind, or disposes it so much for the knowledge of God. But he, who in the spirit of ancient monachism, sits like ' patience on a monument,' assaying to nourish his religious affections by analyzing them, instead of engaging in the active service of his Divine Master, lays a suicidal hand upon himself.

The Bible is, or should be in the hands of every individual of a Christian congregation. And this is the text-book of the minister of the

Gospel. It is God's message to every soul. And it is the minister's business to make that message appreciated and felt—to expound its truths, pour them upon the mind, and drive them home to the heart and conscience of every individual. And if he does not make his hearers feel, that himself is in earnest, and that God is in earnest, so that they shall go away burdened and uncomfortable under the responsibility of their own delinquency, there is a fault in him. A minister and his Church really awake, and in earnest, uniformly demonstrating their prayerfulness and watchfulness for souls, cannot fail to make a corresponding impression upon the world of unbelievers around them.

But these are *general* endeavours—needful and important, as the grand artillery of truth, perpetually pouring forth its thunders on the ears of a sleeping world. These, however, are not enough. They must be followed up by more particular ministrations. The effect should be expected, and watched, and improved. Private preaching should tread upon the heels of public preaching. Tenderness of conscience should be searched out, and cultivated, and made more tender. Every symptom of awakening should be pushed and crowded by still more awakening considerations, so long as the signs of penitence are wanting. The soul of the sinner awakened should not be soothed and comforted, till God comforts it—till it cannot help but be comforted. It is impossible the conscience should be too hardly pressed with truth. Let it writhe and agonize, till the heart surrenders—till the heart breaks into penitence, and relieves itself of its own insupportable burdens, by falling into that condition of submission to God, which the Gospel enjoins. And then the work is done. The soul is comforted, because it cannot help it. It may seek after tears, but it cannot find them. Let man do his part, and God will take care of his.—Let man seek the conversion of sinners, and true conversion will demonstrate itself.

We are speaking of the means of originating revivals of religion; and a revival of religion, let it be kept in mind, is a grand public excitement on the subject of religion. We are not now discussing the expediency of a revival: that is assumed. It is the *means*. The minister must be roused—the Church must be roused —and impenitent sinners must be compelled to feel that the minister and Christians are in earnest for their salvation—that much prayer is offered up, and unwearied efforts exhausted for their immediate return to God. The violated law of God must speak its thunders from the pulpit. The pulpit of the sanctuary must have its auxiliary pulpit in the domestic circle; and the minister must step from the former into the latter, ' visiting from house to house.' He must stand directly in the face of individuals, for a more intimate converse with and deep searching out of their hearts—convincing them that he seeks only the salvation of their souls. ' In season and out of season' he must labour, in public and in private—and his associated flock must labour with him, and hold up his hands— and all together must be found habitually at the throne of Divine grace. It is there they will get their own proper qualifications—the proper spirit ; and there they make an interest with Him, who alone can grant them the thing they desire and seek after.

And with this spirit reigning in the heart of a Christian minister, and in the heart of a church, studying, and praying, and striving together for this one object, they will naturally devise some extraordinary measures. In this let a prudent regard be had to the state and circumstances of their community. Public opinion is not to be disregarded,* even though it be erroneous and corrupt. For if that be shocked, by any course of extraordinary measures, one of the most effectual doors to the hearts of the people is shut. Such was always the wisdom of Paul—' He became all things to all men, if by any means he might save some.' I do not speak here of a compromise of principle,—that can never be allowed, and is never necessary. Expediency, in things indifferent, is the subject. Extraordinary measures for promoting revivals, which have been apparently useful in one place, or in one country, are not of course fit for another, in all the exactitude of their forms. Some might be altogether improper, at least inexpedient, for a foreign application. The state of society, manners and customs, and public opinion, assume such different shapes in different sections of the same country, especially in different nations, that they who stubbornly disregard these accidents, in the institution of extraordinary measures for the revival of religion, are doubtless indiscreet, and likely to be

* Neither is it to be winked at, if it be wrong. It must be treated and acted upon with prudence, as the surest way of eformation.

defeated. Common judgment and good sense, presiding over a proper spirit, is all the rule that can be given.

Prayer is always proper—social prayer and public prayer, and that too for the conversion of sinners. Nobody can object to this, who does not object to all religion. There may be public prayer in the morning, and in the evening, and that too of every day. Look at the altars of the most formal churches in Christendom, habitually lighted up in the morning and evening of every day of the year—and a large part of the year to *prevent* the dawning of the morning, as well as to commune with the shades of the evening. And so long as we can read ' the hour cometh, *and now is*, when the true worshippers shall worship the Father in spirit and in truth,—for the Father seeketh such to worship him ;'—seeketh such, without regard to place and circumstance—whether they stand in the temple at Jerusalem, or whether they be in Samaria—whether it be in the consecrated church, or in the school-room, or in the private mansion, or under the open vault of heaven,—so long we will not trouble ourselves to inquire whether the place of prayer has been set apart for this specific purpose by the superstitious rituals of men. The world, the universe, is consecrated to prayer, and to the worship of God, if the heart be consecrated.

Let Christians who desire a revival of religion, assemble any where, and at any time, as most convenient, and pray for it. Let them meet as often as every day, if there is a spirit to support it; but not otherwise. Let them open the chapel, or the church, for such prayer, every morning and every evening, if there is a demand for it ; but not otherwise. Too frequent public prayer meetings, if unfrequented, will quench, rather than revive the spirit of prayer. Extra-ordinary measures for the revival of religion should not be in advance of the spirit to support them. It would only be disastrous and fatal to the object ; they had better be in rear. Let the spirit fill out the measures, and over-leap them, if it will ; better so than be deficient. The heavy course and inefficient flagging of extraordinary effort will be discouraging. All the *forms* of extraordinary measures should be wisely, and prudently, and prayerfully adopted. The spirit is the thing ; and that is born and must be cherished in the closet. And wher-ever the spirit exists, and in whomsoever, it will be felt.

Let a minister and his church be possessed of and demonstrate the spirit I have described—let their influence, in all proper and convenient ways, address itself to and reach the hearts and consciences of the impenitent:—and sinners will be awakened—will be converted. I do not believe it ever failed; but it will not, of course, amount to a revival: they may be only insulated conversions. A revival, properly so, and in the sense in which I use the term all along, is more than such an excitement as I have just described. It is more than a revival in the heart of a minister and his church, exciting them to special effort, and resulting in the conversion of sinners, more or less, so long as those conversions are only insulated. It is a special and manifest *outpouring* of the Spirit of God, when the work no longer labours in the hands of man, but seems to be taken up of God himself; and God comes down, in a manner and with an influence, before which the wicked stand in awe, and all the people feel his special presence. Awakened sinners may be found in every place, and at every corner. The people are seen rushing in unwonted crowds and under the deepest solemnity to the house of prayer, and to the appointed places of public worship, however frequent; and the exigencies of such a time demand them to be frequent. And the assemblies are still as the grave, and solemn as eternity. Every body hears, because they come to hear—every body feels, because they cannot help it. Every day sinners are awakened, and every day sinners are converted. While one is weeping for his sins, another is rejoicing in hope. And ministers and experienced Christians give themselves up entirely to the work, which God has thrown upon their hands, to warn those who are yet careless, to guide the inquiring, and to nourish those who are born again. Conscience is almost universally tender. Turn where you will to speak of the things of eternity, and you may find a willing ear—address whom you will on the concerns of his soul, and not unlikely the first word will open a fountain of tears. And what is all this? and whence comes it? It is the Spirit of God—it is the power of the Highest —and all feel that it is so. It is a special and a remarkable visitation—a peculiar and striking dispensation of mercy.

It is not, therefore, simply a revived state of feeling in a minister and his church, or among

Christians generally, that constitutes what I mean by a revival of religion; nor, of course, when in addition to, and in consequence of this, there are a few conversions, or even a larger number. This is, indeed, comparatively a revival. But it is not that peculiar and marked dispensation, by the overwhelming influence of which the presence of the Spirit of God is so indubitably certified, overshadowing and involving a whole community simultaneously in the same atmosphere of feeling, and apparently through the medium of the sympathetic affections of our nature. Such a season is the great harvest time of the people and the Church of God.

As *one* of the means of originating revivals, and with the specification of which, perhaps, I ought to have begun, as most of all indispensable—without which, indeed, no others will be effectually employed—is a faith in the *doctrine*—in the possibility, the importance, and the reality of the thing. Here, indeed, is the starting point—this is the means of all other means, standing in the relation of parent to the rest. There must be a faith of the *specific* thing—not a general and vague notion of we know not exactly what. Else how can one know what he is after, what he prays for, what he is trying to bring about? Else how can Christians know when their prayers are answered, and their efforts crowned with success? I do not doubt, indeed, that God, in his sovereignty, may bestow this very thing, in answer to the importunate wrestlings of his faithful servants, while they themselves have no distinct view of it—having had no such experience. I believe that God has done so, and is accustomed to do so, whenever these events occur in advance of experience. Such apparently was the character of these dispensations in the United States, when they first commenced, one hundred years ago. Such, substantially, was their character for a long protracted period, for ages—at least, so far as the intelligent, active, and energetic employment of direct instrumentality is concerned. The people of God in those regions knew what to pray for long time before they had learned how to go to work, as instruments. Hence the long protracted and almost exclusive prevalence of what I have elsewhere denominated the first class of revivals— viz., where the instrumentality was not obvious. And it may be said, that it has taken nearly one hundred years for the American churches to be *schooled* in revivals*—to learn how, as instruments, to originate and promote them. And they have much to learn yet. Indeed, they have but just begun to learn. They are even now constantly making mistakes for want of experience. But experience ripens every year and every day. And I know not why, with adequate experience, such, as I believe, the providence of God will yet throw into the lap of his people—I know not why the state of a revival in a community should not be uninterrupted. I know not why it should not exhibit the character of a constant and uniform progression, without knowing decline. I fully believe it will be so. The symptoms of such a state of uninterrupted progression have already been made apparent, in many communities of the United States, where revivals have been longest enjoyed, best understood, and are still most assiduously cultivated. And if this be indeed the genuine character of those remarkable outpourings of the Spirit predicted in prophecy (as I am inclined to believe it is), any one who has ever witnessed them can easily believe and easily see, with what amazing rapidity and power they

* Not that it will take as long for another community : for the experience of one may answer for another

must advance, when once they shall have come into full operation—when once, by the experience of the church, and the necessary revolutions of society, the way of the Lord shall be prepared, and these outpourings of the Spirit shall have attained the summit tide of their influence. Under these views,—views I maintain suggested by experience—there is nothing incredible in the supposition, that a *literal* construction of the prophecy—' a nation shall be born in a day'—is its intended and exact meaning.

But I have somewhat digressed. Yet these thoughts are important to be somewhere presented, and they are not inappropriate in this connexion. I was speaking of the necessity of faith in the *doctrine* of revivals, as a means of originating them—and of faith in the *specific* thing. For although God in his sovereignty may do over and above the direct aims of the prayers and labours of his people—it is equally certain, it is absolutely certain, that when those aims are right, and when they are urged with all the determination and importunity of faith, God will honour them. And we are now speaking, let it be understood, of human instrumentality. We are attempting to specify *means* of originating revivals—such as are palpable to men—such as are to be employed by men. And I aver, that faith in the doctrine—in the specific thing, is greatly, primarily important.

I have before intimated, that when this dispensation of revivals first commenced in the United States—then British colonies—there were no definite notions concerning them. The way, the state of society was prepared for them, and God was pleased to begin them. I have also intimated, that for a long period, for ages even, the people of God, not doubting they were the special power of God, fully reposed their faith in them, as such—but exhausted their faith in prayer; and then stopped. They had indeed after experience, some definite notions of the thing, and continued to pray for it. But they did not imagine that any duty was incumbent on them, as active instruments. They prayed—and then waited. Hence the slow progress of revivals for so long time. But of late years faith in revivals has not only become more definite—more accordant with the thing—but it has attained a comparative maturity—become enlarged and more practical. It has grown into a living, active, energetic principle, not to expire in the breath of prayer, but taking prayer as its starting point. And scores of ministers, and thousands of gifted and influential Christians, trained by the providence of God in the midst of revivals, and filled with their spirit, have learned to go out ' into the streets and lanes of the city, into the highways and hedges' of the country, ' and *compel* them to come in.' They *believe* in revivals. They have seen them. They have felt them. And they have no more doubt of their reality, than of the shining of the sun, when it is day—or of the moon and stars, when it is night. And they believe too, that man may be the successful instrument of originating them—they see it is the fact—their own experience has proved it. And they go to work with as full and as undoubting confidence, as men apply themselves to any enterprise whatever, in the career of which they have realised repeated and uniform earnests of success. And I believe it will prove true upon examination, and that we may have the uniform testimony of thousands of American Christians, that just in proportion to the amount, decision, and active energy of faith in revivals, has been the success of those, who have devoted themselves to this work, as instruments. Diffidence as to the reality of revivals, as to their genuineness, as the fruit of the Holy Spirit, and an apprehension of their consequences—so as not only to hang in doubt of them, but to be afraid of them—is as fatal to their occurrence, as the damps and chills of death, so far as human instrumentality is concerned. God may come, in *spite* of all this,—even though this diffidence and these apprehensions reign in the heart of a minister and of his Church—God may still come, and confound their diffidence, and chase away their apprehensions, and make them willing in the day of his power. So, I believe, God has done, in instances not a few. But we are now speaking of human instrumentality, such as is obvious—such as originates in man's own heart, and lies in his own power—such, as experience abundantly proves, may be applied with success. And the very root, and the living spring of that instrumentality, in all its diversified ramifications, is *faith*—a faith in the *doctrine*, comprehending some definite notion of the thing.

I might go into very extended enumeration of the specific forms of extraordinary measures, which have been devised and employed in the

United States for the promotion of revivals of religion—and many of them with eminent, distinguished success. But I do not think it very material. I think, indeed, it might be even disadvantageous, if they were to be adopted indiscriminately, in another country, without paying regard to the different conditions of society, to different customs and manners, which must consequently induce a different combination of the moral elements. Some of those measures would probably prove unfortunate, if adopted in England;—and some of them, in my opinion, are equally applicable in any part of the world, because they are founded in human nature, and not in the accidental conditions of society.

Of the latter class are prayer meetings, special and frequent, having specifically in view a revival of religion;—a public definition of the different classes and grades of impenitent sinners, so exact and graphic, that they shall feel themselves described and addressed, charging home upon them their guilt and responsibility;—an actual and public separation, in some form, and occasionally, of believers from unbelievers—of those who are willing to profess Christ before the world from those who are not—of the anxious from those who are unconcerned, all with great prudence, selecting carefully the time and circumstance, and yet so striking and so impressive, and with such accompanying appeals, as are likely to be felt ;—immediate, direct, and personal addresses to impenitent sinners, with a view to ascertain the state of their minds, and urge them to repentance by the solemn sanctions of religion, and be sure to reach their conscience ;—a use of the state of the public mind on the subject of religion, declaring what it is and what it ought to be—if it is stupid, thunder upon it—if it is awakened, urge on the awakening ;—if it is highly excited, announce in the ears of all, with irresistible earnestness, ' now is the accepted time, now is the day of salvation ;' and many other efforts of this description, as wisdom, in view of circumstances, may dictate.

Of the public division of a religious assembly, or a separation of its classes, I beg leave to speak more particularly—as it is a very delicate and momentous measure, and should be used with the greatest prudence. One of these divisions is common, in all parts of the world,—

when professing Christians come to the Lord's table. And I do not hesitate to say, that this ordinance ought to be celebrated in such circumstances, as to detain the unbelieving portion of a congregation as spectators. Here then is a division, and what an opportunity of appeal! It is a division made without violence, by a common sense of propriety, and above all others combines circumstances of the most affecting and overwhelming considerations! Who could resist them, if rightly improved?

It is extensively a custom in churches of the United States, for all persons who have been approved as candidates for the Lord's table, or for what is ordinarily termed admission into full communion of the church, to present themselves before the whole congregation on the day of the sacramental supper, and there publicly make a profession of their faith, by assenting to certain questions, propounded by the officiating minister, and also to enter into a formal and public covenant with God and his people. And this is a division, or separation, and a very solemn and impressive one, not only to the candidates, but to all the witnesses. It is often of amazing and incalculable power, and probably never without some deep impression. I will here narrate a scene of this kind, of which I was once the witness.

It was after a season of some considerable revival, when on a sacramental sabbath, fifty-one of the converts, male and female, old and young, and in some instances parents with their children, presented themselves, at the call of their aged and venerable pastor, in the broad aisle of the church, standing in ranks before all the congregation, and directly in front of the pulpit, and of the communion-table. The house was filled to overflowing, with a mixed multitude of believers and unbelievers—but all interested, all gazing at the scene, enacting before them, with an intensity of interest, which cannot be described—for the Spirit of God was there. It was a season of revival. These fifty one persons had now, and in these circumstances publicly separated themselves from the world, there to take the vows of God upon them, in the presence of God, of angels, and of this multitude of witnesses on earth, and then to sit down together, and for the first time to receive the consecrated symbols of a Saviour's dying love.

And the venerable patriarch, their pastor and

spiritual father, descending from the pulpit, took his station behind the Communion-table, supported on either hand by his elders and deacons, and was about to proceed to the installation of these waiting candidates in the fellowship and privileges of the church. For a moment all was silence and rapt attention, while that aged man of God stood struggling to arm his tongue for utterance. The sympathies of all hearts clustered round him, as he was seen labouring in vain to express his emotions. At last, with a trembling and broken voice, addressing himself to the officers and members of his church, and looking upon this fresh company now coming up, to offer themselves to God, he delivered himself of this brief sentence : ' This is the day, and this the hour, my brethren, which I have long wished, and prayed, and laboured to see.' And the old man could say no more. But, turning himself, he fell upon the shoulder of one of the elders, who stood by his side, and wept aloud. And the whole congregation were instantly possessed of the same feeling, and equally convulsed by the uncontrollable power of their emotions.

Like an elder father, and an elder saint, who

on a more joyful occasion took the infant Saviour in his arms, and was satisfied—so did this venerable man, bending alike under the weight of years, and alike hoary with the whitened locks of a care-worn life—so did he, as soon as he could lift himself up again, raise his trembling hands, and streaming eyes, and faltering voice to heaven, breaking once more the protracted pause and awful silence of the place:—' Now lettest thou thy servant depart in peace—for mine eyes have seen thy salvation.'

And never will that hour be forgotten by those who witnessed the scene. And its impression on that Church and on that people will last, while they shall last—while eternity lasts. And names, I trust not a few, I cannot doubt, will be found in heaven, in consequence of the impressions of that occasion.

Such is sometimes the amazing and overwhelming power of the division of a religious congregation. And a congregation may be divided on other occasions, and for other purposes. But if it be a device, and out of the common order, it ought to be done with supreme discretion, and rarely. In various forms, and among other means, it has doubtless been made a great, useful, and powerful expedient in promoting revivals of religion.

There is one in extensive and habitual use in the United States, which it may be proper to mention and describe, though it is but a few years since it was introduced. It is called the *anxious seat*. Although it came into use in seasons of revival, and has been principally employed on those occasions, it is not exclusively confined to that use. It is often employed as a means of *originating* a revival, and sometimes with great success. Ordinarily it is reserved for the extra seasons of public worship—for evening services, and the public prayer meeting room, where the exact order of stated ordinances is not considered so important to be observed. The use of it is left in the discretion of the officiating minister, or ministers,—and it is not considered prudent to employ it, except when there is manifestly a special degree of feeling in the congregation. On such occasions, and ordinarily towards the close of the meeting, a challenge is formally made on all those, who are willing publicly to signify their anxiety to secure an interest in the great salvation—to separate themselves from the congregation, and come and be seated by themselves, that public prayer may be offered in their behalf, and that they may receive suitable advice and exhortation. And by this act they are known as inquirers, and treated as such, so long as they desire, or need it. None are likely to comply with this invitation, except those whose anxiety is paramount to their fear of the world, and of public observation. And every body is aware that such must be the feeling—such the overpowering impulse, which constrains obedience to such a call. And no matter how often it has been done—no matter though it be a thing of every day—yet every recurrence of the same scene produces substantially the same effect, both on a congregation and on those who go forward.

The individual who rises for such a purpose, is apt to be so overwhelmed as to be unable to reach the place, without the guidance and support of a second person; and immediately the sympathies of the whole congregation, except those who are hardened and resolved in sin, are roused to unwonted energy. A second, and a third, and perhaps a large number rise, one after another, and press forward, under the same

emotions, to the same place. And the common feeling increases. The anxious seat is filled; and they, and the congregation with them, are in tears. The minister rises, and asks :—' And are there no more ? No more ? None others in this congregation resolved to renounce the world, and seek after heaven ? None others here who feel their need of a Saviour ? Dare you wait till to-morrow ? To-morrow, remember, is the thief of time, and the grave of souls.'*
And another, and perhaps another, and it may be yet a number, press forward to claim a place with those, whose example has decided them. And now the offer is suspended, and fervent, importunate prayers are offered up in behalf of these anxious souls, who kneel weeping before the altar of God. And the congregation weep with them. And they are counselled, exhorted, and dismissed. But their names are known, and they are not forgotten, or neglected. And the effect of this step on those, who thus present themselves, ordinarily is a speedy conversion. The amazing power of the circumstances, instrumentally, and the Spirit of God accompanying, bring their feelings—enforce them to the

* Not of course in this exact language, but the minister is accustomed to make some such use of the occasion.

crisis of submission to God. And the effect upon the community is great. It is sometimes the means of originating, and always the means of promoting a revival.

There are various other modes of dividing a public religious assembly, which have sometimes been blessed, though somewhat hazardous, and not in common use. In proportion as they are uncommon, is there need of the greatest prudence. A new experiment of this description is always momentous, and in the hands of the indiscreet, dangerous. I happened the last summer, on a great religious occasion of several days continuance, in the Valley of the Mississippi, to be a witness of the division of a public assembly in a somewhat novel form—at least so far as I know. It took every body by surprise, and yet was very felicitous, and impressive beyond imagination to conceive. I here offer a brief account of it.

It was the third or fourth day of a great religious convocation—-occasions not unfrequent in the United States, and got up as a kind of Missionary and revival effort, bringing together ministers, and Christians, and people from an extensive region round about,—and extraordinary principally, as being an extraordinary and protracted concentration of ordinary means on the public mind. The influence of these occasions is to combine more advantageously, to raise and concentrate the moral power of the Church upon a wider region, than an ordinary congregation—to collect representatives of numerous churches and congregations, and of all their classes,—to reap the advantage of the natural excitement of a great public assembly for religious purposes,—to call into action and improve the various gifts of the ministry under these rare and interesting combinations of society,—to support continuously for a number of days a powerful concentration of religious effort on an extended portion of the public mind, and bringing to bear on a single point the united power of a large number of associated ministers, whose various gifts and qualifications, succeeding each other, keep expectation alive, and naturally augment the excitements of such an occasion.

On one of the days of such a convocation, and during an interval, when those services, in which a regular sermon is expected, were suspended, as is common at these times, and for the sake of keeping the attention of the people variously, yet profitably occupied, what is called a prayer.

meeting was held. And at some hours these meetings are as full as those for a sermon. The order of these meetings is not uniform, and is left in the discretion of the ministers who happen to preside. In the present instance the presiding minister was a man of great mental resource, of much experience, long practised in revivals, full of useful expedient, rarely missing his aim, and enjoying public confidence to an unlimited extent. When the assembly were all seated before him, he took occasion to address himself to Christian parents, in reference to their children, who had been dedicated to God in baptism, and yet remained unconverted, in some such language as the following :—' What are the reasons?—Do you use all proper means? —Do you pray for them ?—Do you pray *with* them, so as to make them interested ?—Do you make them feel, in your treatment of them, that you are concerned for their salvation ?—Suppose we make a season of special prayer for these children, who are now here with you.—And for this purpose, let room be made in all the seats immediately before and around the pulpit, and let all Christian parents, who are here to-day, bring their children, older or younger, and here solemnly renew the consecration of them to God, and pray that God would now by his Spirit, *this day—this hour,* effectually impress their hearts, and bring them to repentance. And there are, doubtless, some of your children here, who have come to a maturity of years, or are found in the buoyant days of youth, yet unconverted, who will be surprised at this call, and may feel reluctant to comply with your wishes. I say then to all such :—If you are willing to be deprived of the benefit of these prayers, if you are prepared to say to God thus publicly, and in this manner, that you " *will* none of these things—that you will not have Christ to reign over you "—then stay back. If you are willing thus to disappoint and afflict the hearts of your parents, then stay back. But remember you are now to make an eventful choice—a choice, which may carry you to heaven, or send you to hell. Come, then, Christian parents with your baptised children, and we will here offer up our fervent and united prayers to heaven, that they may *this day* be baptised with the Holy Ghost.'

I do not pretend to give the language, I only present the argument. And immediately the congregation began to move. Place was given, as requested. And Christian parents began to take up their children, bringing some in their arms, and leading others by their side. Some of the children declined the wishful looks and heart-appealing expressions of their parents, and obliged their parents to go forward without them, weeping as they went. But most of them only stayed to sink down overwhelmed, not only with a sense of their unfilial conduct, but it is to be hoped also with a sense of the fearful choice they had made, and to regret it in the bitterness of their souls. An interesting company, indeed, of parents and children, in these interesting circumstances, and for such an object, stood up in that place. What a scene! How novel! And yet how befitting! How proper! Who could say, it was improper—when it was all so decent, so orderly, so affecting?—And what Christian would not have found it happiness to be there, to weep in such an assembly, at such a sight?—Never, probably, did Christian parents feel more the agony of concern and the agony of prayer for the salvation of their children. And never, perhaps, were a group of baptised children placed in a situation, where the concentrated influences of parental and Christian solicitude bore upon them with more subduing power. And it was more than evident, that they felt it. Parents and children were affectionately addressed and admonished, and prayers, with a holy unction and fervent importunity, went up to heaven in their behalf. Nothing was more manifest, than the presence and power of the Holy Spirit, throughout the assembly, as well as among this interesting group.

The occasion was altogether too felicitous and too impressive, not to suggest a farther improvement by other expedients. Immediately, as the objects of this especial grouping of Christian parents with their children, were attained, the *anxious seat*, as before described, was prepared. And now, the baptised children separately, and any others, whose anxious concern might urge them to such a step, were invited to come forward, and confess their solicitude before the world, and receive the advice, and prayers, and benedictions of God's ministers, and of his people. And instantly they came, in a flock, weeping as they came, and to the number of forty, or more, as nearly as I remember, placed themselves in that conspicuous and interesting

spot. They were generally of adult years—*all*
old enough to have been sinners, to need repentance, and an interest in Christ.

And among the rest came two twin-sisters,
about fourteen years of age, arm in arm, and
took their seat—their heads bowed down, and
their hearts full of sorrow for their sins. They
were born into the world in company, always
lived in company, alike in all respects; accustomed to sympathize on all subjects and on all
occasions, they sympathized now. They felt
together their need of a Saviour, and came
together soliciting of the ministers and people
of God their advice and prayers.

' What shall *we* do to be saved ? ' They were
the daughters of an elder in one of the churches,
who, but a moment before, had stood with them,
and wept over them, and prayed for them, in this
very place. Surprised with joy at this unexpected manifestation of such feelings, he could
not refrain from making some effort to speak
with them. As they sat upon their seat, their
heads bowed low in grief, and supporting each
other, their father approached, and as a matter
of convenience, kneeled down upon one of his
knees to get their attention. The moment they

perceived it was their father, they fell simultaneously upon his neck, one upon one shoulder
and the second upon the other, his head between
theirs, and each throwing an arm about the
father's neck; and in that situation the father
and his twin daughters remained, as if chained
together, and wept, and wept, and wept. And all
who witnessed the scene gave themselves up to
tears. And those dear children, born into the
world in one hour, in one hour apparently were
born into the kingdom of God. And what a pic-
ture! It was a sight, which angels might covet to
see, and doubtless did see it—and winged with
joy their way to heaven to announce the intel-
gence;—a sight, which perhaps was never presented before, and probably never will be again,
in a form so interesting, so affecting, so subduing!

But I did not intend by this case of the twin-
daughters, a mere accident of the whole scene, as
it was, to withdraw attention from the principal
consideration—the moral, and sometimes useful
effect of dividing a religious assembly, if it be
done with great prudence. But it is not to be
risked in indiscreet hands. The effect, in the
instance just narrated, was altogether felicitous

and overpowering. All such arrangements must be left in the discretion, and imposed on the responsibility of the ministers of religion—allowing that they are desirous of doing any thing proper and expedient for the revival of religion.

One thing is certain, that *extra* efforts and *extra* measures, in some form, are indispensable to a revival, so far as they are to be brought about and promoted by human instrumentality. The Christian and religious world soon get asleep, and are sure to sleep on, with nothing but the same wonted round of a formal religious service to act upon them. It is not in human nature, and I had almost said, it is not in grace to rise above it. And all other things being equal, the religious stupor of the public mind will grow stronger and stronger every day, every year, and every generation, in the same dull round of religious formality—until all spiritual life be swallowed up in the cares of the world and the corruptions of our nature. To use the plainest language possible—the world, the Church itself continually requires some fresh and rousing impulse. It needs to be *waked up*. It requires occasional recurrence of some novel com-

binations of the moral and religious forces to
act upon it, and to act with a startling energy—
and that just in proportion as the tendencies of
human nature go to let attention to religion
flag. Until the Church, until Christians shall
learn this lesson, they are equally deficient in
their attainments towards the true philosophy of
Christianity, as of human nature. And so long
as they fear a new movement in the religious
world, *because* it is new, they are in little danger
of a revival of religion, if that is the thing,
which of all others they fear most. Let ministers and churches be possessed of the proper
spirit, a spirit of ardent, unyielding, untiring
purpose for the revival of religion,—let them
see (*philosophically*, if it must be called so—for
that is true philosophy, which discovers the real
causes of defeat and the best means of success
in every enterprise)—let them see, that *extra*
efforts and *extra* measures are indispensable,—
and then let their best and holiest discretion be
taxed for the invention and the application of
means and measures. God forbid they should
run with headlong and blind impetuosity into
hasty, unadvised, unproved expedients. The
particular *form* of extra measures, as I have

before sufficiently intimated, should always have respect to the conditions of society where they are introduced. To disregard such considerations would be to set aside one of the most important talents, for the right use of which God has made us responsible—and that is *discretion.*

Protracted religious solemnities, continued from day to day, bringing together a large representation of the ministers, and churches, and people of an extended region, have proved of great service in the United States, as means of originating and promoting revivals. Such occasions will of course collect the best spirits and the weight of piety both from the ministry and from the churches. The ardour of one kindles that of another, and the contact of fervent spirits increases the fervour of all. The intercourse and fellowship of ministers, of churches, and of Christians generally, when it is projected and cultivated for the very purpose of mutual stimulation to the grand enterprises of the age—when they cannot, and will not find time to trifle—when prayer, and faith, and action are the watch-word—stir up devoted spirits, and make them more devoted. Especially when the spirit of revival is in them—for after all, and in truth, it is a peculiar spirit. A little taste of it creates an appetite for more. It is all on tiptoe—alert, prone to action. It is a diffusive and energetic leaven, pervading and binding together all affinities. These protracted meetings in the United States have originated in this spirit, have been sustained and multiplied by it, and have recreated it. And they are admirably calculated for the purpose ; and the outpourings of the Divine Spirit have often come down in the midst of them, and have often followed them. They embrace a number of days, from three to seven, and the Sacrament of the Lord's Supper is ordinarily a part of the great solemnity, when ministers and churches seem to be pledged anew by a more intimate and more extended association, and under special obligations.

Although I began these specifications of extra efforts, by assuming a supposed case of a minister and church, to whom they are to apply, the general spirit of them, and most of them literally are equally applicable to all possible cases, at least to all common conditions of a community. Wherever religion is low, or in decline, the same efforts substantially are necessary to a revival.

And after all is done, there is nothing more

important, or more necessary, than an humble spirit of dependence on God. A genuine revival of religion is the fruit of the outpouring of the Holy Spirit. And although God honours faithfulness in his servants, he will yet be honoured himself, first and chief. And an essential ingredient of faithfulness, is humility. Christians should use means, as if all depended upon them, and then all their dependence should be upon God. Nothing has been more manifest, in the dispensation of revivals of religion in the United States, than this truth:—that God will certainly disappoint that reliance, which does not reach unto himself. A man, for instance, has been eminently useful in promoting revivals. Let him visit a church and people, who look to him, as they ought to look to God, and they will be disappointed. A particular means has been honoured in one, or more instances, as the apparent instrumentality. And the moment that shall get to have an honour, in the eyes of Christians, as if it were *the* power, God will withdraw his energy, and employ some other means. The tendencies to such dependence are very strong. And the idolatry which Christians sometimes pay to particular means, and to particular measures, and to particular men, is exceedingly injurious to the cause of revivals, and often prevents them altogether. God will be honoured, and will have the glory. And all I have said of the probable success of means and measures, is predicated on the supposition, that they are to be sustained by the proper spirit.

Of the *hindrances* to a revival, I have already spoken incidentally of a want of faith—faith in the doctrine of revivals, and in the energetic application of means. And as this is so important an item, I deem it worthy to be brought up again. It may be noticed, that I have maintained a distinction between God's visitations by his Spirit for the revival of religion, independent of a visible instrumentality, and his visitations by the same influence, and for the same purpose, through the medium of an instrumentality, which is quite apparent. Visitations of the former class may come, when everything seems to be opposed—even when the minister and church are opposed—and nobody seems to desire or seek it. I will not stop to speculate upon such dispensations, although I do not think they are altogether inscrutable—not at all so, indeed, when reference is made to the doctrines of revelation. But I am not now speaking of what God can do, nor of what he may find reasons to do—reasons not so palpable to us. It is the province of duty prescribed to his people, which is now under consideration—and the relations of that duty to results, as they are ordinarily developed in the economy of Divine Providence. And upon this basis, I say, that diffidence and apprehension concerning revivals of religion, in those who ought to be leaders in the cause of Christ, are apt to be insuperable obstacles to their occurrence—and will be so, so far as their instrumentality is concerned. I assume, that revivals of religion are the genuine fruit of God's Spirit—and that there is such a thing, as *grieving* and *quenching* the spirit, *publicly* as well as individually. Christians must not be *afraid* of God's Spirit—they must not be afraid, that God's Spirit will do mischief —that it will derange their arrangements—discompose the order of things, which they have established, or which they might imagine is best. They must not be afraid, that it will make too much work for them—that it will summon them from their easy couches into the field of action, and expose them to greater hardships. So long as such are their apprehensions, they may rest assured, they will not be disturbed—unless the time has come, when, for reasons independent of their will and agency, God has resolved to break in upon their repose, and get to himself 'a name and a praise,' in spite of all their oppositions. There is as much need of a *conversion of Christians* into a belief and into the spirit of revivals, as of the world ' dead in trespasses and sins,' into the life of holiness—and ordinarily there is as much *apparent* difference in the change. I have known many ministers, and multitudes of private Christians, after having experienced this conversion, (I beg leave to call it so,) honestly and perseveringly throw away all their former religion, as good for nothing, and adopt the full belief, that their former profession was an empty name;—a hasty and unwarrantable conclusion, I think, and not beneficial in its tendencies,—but yet honest, and not perhaps altogether without reason. Better that they had kept it to themselves, even though they thought so. This change is, however, what I should be strongly inclined to call (could I persuade myself, that such was the meaning of the Apostle) a ' *renewing* of the Holy Ghost,' subsequent to the ' washing of regeneration.' It is a great and striking renewal of the Divine life in the soul. And it is best begotten in the very atmosphere of a revival—and such is ordinarily its birth-place.

But still there may be a *conviction*—a deep, abiding, thorough-working, practical conviction in the doctrine of revivals, itself *generative* of such a state of things instrumentally, before the most thorough renewal of the mind upon this subject has taken place. The mind may be fully satisfied, by a thorough study of the doctrines, and a deep imbibing of the spirit of Christianity—by credible reports of this work of God in other and distant regions—and more than all, by the Spirit of God moving in itself, and vigorously exciting it to habitual salient efforts and holy aspirations after a better state of things—by such influences, the mind may be *fully* satisfied, that there is such an economy of Divine Providence in the dispensations of Divine grace, as is ordinarily represented under the name of revivals of religion. And this is the conviction, which, taking deep root and working thoroughly and habitually in the hearts of ministers and Christians of any community, however foreign to such dispensations in fact of time or place,—exciting them to prayer and untiring effort for the enjoyment of the same blessing among themselves—may be expected to be instrumental in bringing it down from heaven. And just in proportion, as ministers and Christians are diffident upon this subject, and much more, if they are apprehensive of consequences, are they and their people unlikely to be the subjects of such a visitation.

The root of all hindrances, therefore, to a revival of religion, is this want of faith. And as a faith of this kind, in the invention and persevering employment of means, when prevalent and energetic, is likely to triumph over all opposition, I do not think it necessary to go into a specification of the multiplied and varied hindrances, which grow out of the imperfection attaching itself to Christians, lamentable as it is, and out of the depravity developed by the unbelieving world in so many forms.

There is, however, one hindrance, and I may add, *quencher* of revivals, so apt to exist, and so fatal—and yet in the power of Christians to suppress, because it is found in their own breast—

that I cannot forbear to mention it, if possibly I might contribute my own influence with that of others, to fix upon it its own deserved stamp of reprobation, and thus subtract from its power, and aid in driving it from the Church. I mean the spirit of *Sectarianism.* It is the spirit of bigotry—a hateful fiend—a pestilential breath —which has blasted more hopes of the Church than all other influences put together. I have reference to no particular denomination. It is chargeable upon every Christian sect on earth. It is the common vice of human nature:—' I am right, and you are wrong.' Start this spirit against a revival, or in the midst of one, and you have started a foul fiend. You have let loose a demon in his fury, to desolate all your hopes.

Christians of different sects, in the providence of God, ordinarily make parts of the component elements of every considerable community ; and they have their sectarian views, and sectarian rights. Christians of the same sect often differ from each other in some of their theological speculations, and in minor things. And if they do not take care, they are in danger of attaching too much importance to their own peculiar tenets. They may even come to an idolatry of them—and then is an end of usefulness—there beginneth the empire of bigotry. The fact that religious disputants, however conscientious they may profess themselves, are always unhappy, and always produce unhappiness in others;— the fact that the Spirit of God always ' flies from the realms of noise and strife,'—ought to be a sufficient admonition, that God does not approve of a sectarian spirit—that he does not require such a guardianship even of the true faith, and will not accept it.

Some Christians set up a particular sacramental ordinance, as everything ;—some, a doctrine ; some, a particular set of doctrines ;—some require, that a whole system of theology should be understood by a child ;—some imagine, that the true faith and the Church (which of course is always their party) are in danger, by the slightest deviations from the very niceties of their creed, according to their own construction of it, and are ready to take the field with all the earnestness and impetuosity of a Quixote, at sight of the giddy and alarming whirl of a windmill. There is no cure for such a disposition, but heaven. And there is great reason to fear, that in many instances it will never undergo a refinement fit for that place. It will not consent that even the Spirit of God should come into its community, except it shall operate in a particular way, and not disturb the faith of its own assumed protection. The least symptom of deviation will throw it into a fever, and challenge and put in requisition all its officiousness. A sinner may not be converted, unless he can be catechised on a whole system of theology. What a deplorable ignorance of human nature, both in others and in itself, does such a spirit demonstrate! It is to be avoided, and shunned, and let alone, as the pestilence, for all the purposes of originating and promoting a revival of religion. Controversy is death to a revival. As if the Bible were lost to the world, and nothing left but a human creed! As if the Holy Spirit would patronize other than his own inspired truth! As if God were not an adequate guardian of his own cause, when he comes with power to assert it, and to make men fear and love him! As if there were not a harmony in Divine truth, that he, who has received one cardinal principle into his heart, as the instrument of his conversion, were not likely to get hold of the rest by study of the Bible and prayer, and the ordinary course of a Christian education! As if it were not easier to make correct religious thinkers of men after conversion, than before! As if these officious individuals were the sole guardians of faith and of conscience!

I cannot but remark here, that certain theological speculations are apt to have an influence, favourable or unfavourable, to revivals of religion; and also, that this is not a bad test of the probable correctness or incorrectness of such speculations. Any theology, which discourages and quenches the spirit of revivals, may well be regarded as suspicious; and that which fosters and cherishes the spirit, is more likely the theology of the Bible. A system of theology, however, is neither to be abandoned nor adopted by this rule hastily. A correct theology may operate unfavourably in this particular, by holding certain parts of it in distortion—in a sort of caricature—by attaching an undue importance to particular truths, and leaving others in the back ground. And *vice versá* — a theology incorrect in some particulars, may prove comparatively innocent, where the heart is honest, and submits itself to the cardinal doctrines and most practical precepts of Christianity.

———

CHAPTER VIII.

CONSIDERATION OF THE EVILS OF REVIVALS, REAL AND ALLEGED——AND OF SCANDALOUS REPORTS CONCERNING THEM.

' THINK not that I came to send peace on the earth. I came not to send peace, but a sword.' Is this the declaration of a purpose ?—or a mere prediction of results? There can be but one answer to this question, unless they are to be regarded, who speak from malice. Was it expedient that the Son of God should suspend— yea, for ever decline his mission into our world, because it must necessarily call forth human depravity in other and new forms ?—Because human nature is so bad, that God himself could not institute and bring to bear upon it an economy of redemption, without provoking it to the most outrageous assaults upon his benevolence, and abuses of his kindness, should it therefore not be redeemed ?—Because ages on ages, and centuries heaped upon centuries, must roll away, men exhausting their inventions, in the

successive periods of their spiritual enthralment,
to embarrass, impede, and defeat the benevolent
designs of God, in all possible ways, and more
than all in the perversion of Divine institutions,
—before the apparatus of redemption could be
completed, and the necessary revolutions of society prepare the way for its most successful
and thorough operation—was it therefore better,
that the world should remain in eternal bond-
age, and not a single effort be made for relief?—
The answer of these questions, or any one of
them, in view of the reasons on which they are
founded, might, with the greatest propriety,
make the sum and conclusion of this chapter.
For these questions and their answers declare,
in the same breath, the legitimate origin and
the true occasion of all the evils of revivals of
religion. Admit that the application of the
plan of redemption to our world makes men
more outrageous and more violent, than they
would have been under a mere suspension of the
sentence of condemnation, under a probation like
to the present, excepting only this consummation
of its purpose—is this the fault of the remedy,
and of him who brings it in?—Besides, let it be
remembered, that all the kindness of human

nature, all that it falls short of the finished depravities of a fiendly character, is owing to the probation and restraining grace conferred, as a basis for the execution of the scheme of redemption.

Look at the disturbances at Jerusalem, and in the nation of Israel, occasioned by the personal ministry of their Prince and Saviour; and at the terrible consummation, on Calvary, of the persecutions raised against him. And was it not ' by wicked hands,' that he was slain, although ' delivered by the determinate counsel and foreknowledge of God?' And what a fearful concussion of the moral elements of society did the very outset of the ministry of the apostles produce, accompanied as it was by the Holy Ghost sent down from heaven! They, and their coadjutors, and their immediate successors convulsed the Roman empire, throughout its vast extent, and to its very throne. The apostles were constituted the pioneers of Christianity. The mightiest conflict, which the world has ever suffered, or probably ever will suffer, between true and false religion, was vested in their hands. So utterly opposed was the state of the world to the principles of Christianity, that the latter went well nigh to the dissolution of society and its reorganization. And yet can any Christian pronounce that grand convulsion an undesirable event—an evil?

And then look at the history of the corruptions of Christianity, for a long series of ages, the end of which cannot be seen even at this late day, only by the glass of prophecy. And God grant it may soon come. See the beginning, and mark the growing up—the gradual accretion—of that huge, unsightly, and deformed mass of superstition, which has buried and choked beneath its rubbish the soul of Christianity, and bound society in chains, and checked its progress, for so many centuries;—attaining spiritual oppression by such diabolical devices and inhuman cruelties, as to [have shocked humanity, and frightened half the world from the hope, and almost from the desire, of emancipation;—so as to have caused the charge to be lodged at the door of Christianity, of being the occasion of more bloodshed, of more evil, and of more calamity to the human race, than all other causes combined. And is this a just charge?—Is Christianity, indeed, accountable for all this?—And will any man presume to implead the author of this religion, and bring his accusation before the throne of heaven, for having disturbed the peace and order of human society, and inflicted on the human family a long and painful series of the direst calamities, with which the world has ever been visited ?

And look at the sectarian branches, and sad divisions, and angry controversies, which have grown out of the Protestant Reformation,—itself, in all its forms, needing to be reformed. And is that not a blessing—is that to be reckoned an evil to the world ? Are these consequences the legitimate fruits of the principles of the Reformation ? Is the Reformation to be made re sponsible for all the faults of any, who may be found in its ranks ?—Or, are not the true causes rather to be found in the vices of human nature ?

But to come to the point. Of course I can only speak of the history of revivals in the United States. I have already alluded to the entire want of experience in public excitements of this kind, when they first made their appearance in New England one hundred years ago, and allowed, that they suffered a long protracted and painful decline, in consequence of the mismanagement, and of more or less extravagance, which grew out of that want of experience. But the worst of the mismanagement, and the worst shapes of extravagance, were not so considerable, or remarkable, as to be worthy of record for any other purpose, than as beacons for future advice. It is admitted on all hands, that the church was greatly enlarged and edified — that Christian character was improved, and the standard of piety elevated—that the interests of society generally were promoted and advanced—and that a new and vigorous impulse was imparted to Christian enterprise, which has never lost its force, and which constituted the basis of that high and notable character of the Christian world, in the United States, which has been erected upon it within a generation past. The Christian historians of that early and first age of revivals, of whom none is more venerable, or more worthy of credit, than President Edwards, have left sufficient records upon the subject to demonstrate the extensive and thorough reformations, which were then produced in very many communities throughout New England, and in some other parts of the colonies. And they have staked their reputation, in vouching to their character, as the genuine fruit of the Holy Spirit. And no one can doubt their fidelity in recording the more disagreeable features of those excitements, in making a fair presentation of the whole case. Take for instance the narratives of President Edwards:—and there you see the artless simplicity of the child, the conscientiousness of the Christian, the unadulterated holiness of the man of God, the sagacity of the philosopher, and the scrupulous fidelity of the historian, all combined in such winning and attractive forms, that you cannot entertain a doubt, either of the honesty of his heart, of the minuteness and exactitude of his information, or of the soundness of his judgement. You will feel not only that this man believed what he tells you, but that he tells you the truth,—and that his opinion of the facts in question is worthy of the greatest respect. And what is that opinion? It is soberly and unhesitatingly, that these revivals were the work of God's Holy Spirit. And he demonstrates it by the exuberance, and extent, and character of their fruits—after deducting all the bad things, which had a contemporaneous existence, in the relation of vice to virtue,—having as little and no other alliance, except that they often stand side by side in the same field.

Honesty requires the admission, that about thirty years ago a very extensive religious excitement prevailed over extensive regions of the valley of the Mississipi, in the United States, coming up to the Alleghany ridge on the East,— and, in some instances, passing that boundary,— which, for the want of an experienced and skilful ministry, and in the hands of ignorant men, produced some very disastrous results. But that excitement has always been reckoned one of its own class and alone. It has not commonly been ranked among revivals of religion in the United States, except only as it has been mentioned by itself. And to this day, it has been matter of the gravest doubt, whether it be worthy of the name. And yet, notwithstanding all the wildness and extravagancies, for which it was remarkable, there seem to have been planted germs in the midst of it, which have since grown up into more sober stocks, and have borne much good fruit; which would seem to justify the conclusion, that the Spirit of God might have been there, and its richest and best fruits only prevented by the introduction and prevalence of a blind and over-heated enthusiasm. I have been credibly informed, by one of the colloquists of a grave discussion on this subject, between one of our most prominent and influential statesmen, who had spent his active life upon the premises, except when called away on affairs of state, and another most respectable gentleman alike qualified to speak,—that, when they came to an expression of opinion, they both agreed, that when the chaff had all blown away, there remained much wheat;—and this statesman, who made no profession of religion, nor any pretension of an experimental acquaintance with it, confessed, that he had no philosophy within his reach to account for these results, and for the character demonstrated by these men, independent of the Christian doctrine of the agency of the Holy Spirit. So that after all, it would appear, that the character of Christianity has not suffered in the view of sensible men, even where religion has shown itself under such great disadvantages. But I would not notice such a dispensation for any other purpose, than to clear away the clouds, which rest upon it. I would never myself become the advocate of such a revival of religion. And I do not consider, that it has any just claim to be classed among those occurrences, which I have all along had in view, and which I rank under this denomination.

I have known many public religious excitements, of a limited extent, which I could not allow to be genuine revivals of religion—characterized by a forced state of feeling, transient in duration, and meagre in its fruits—and those fruits of a doubtful character. While, however, I would not be considered as delivering a grave opinion of religious excitements, with which I have not been conversant,—that only excepted upon which I have already pronounced,—I wish to be understood, as advocating, in this work, that class of revivals, *particularly*, which made their first appearance in New England in the days of President Edwards; which have continued from that time without interruption, though not without decline; and which have been growing up and multiplying to a most interesting extent, within the past generation, and spreading themselves recently over widely extended territories of the United States. And these revivals are exactly the same now, that they were a hundred years ago—with this exception, that the instrumentality of them at present is more apparent, and is made a subject of deep study and systematic application. And it is my opinion of *such* revivals, for the expression of which I hold myself responsible to the world, and to God.

Take these revivals, then, as they have existed in New England generally, and still show themselves there—take them, as they have gradually been extending and growing up for many years in the States of New York, New Jersey and Ohio; and as not altogether unknown in many other parts of the Union—and I will not fear to become their advocate before all the world, as the production of no other power, than the special agency of the almighty Spirit of the eternal God. And I should hope to show, too, that they are worthy of God;—that they are worthy, not only of the confidence of the Christian world, but of the respect of all mankind.

That there are strong tendencies to irregularities, and to extravagant exhibitions of human passion, in the deep excitement and powerful agitation of the public mind on any subject, everybody knows. And it were not to be supposed, knowing as we all do the vices of human nature, that when the souls of congregated masses of human beings are once stirred up to reflection on the momentous themes of religion —themes more than any other calculated to bring into action all the passions of the soul, under their intensest energies—it were not to be supposed, I say, that the vices of human nature, in such circumstances, will not show themselves. He is a weak philosopher, and wanting in common discernment, who could not make allowance for the occurrence of undesirable things at such a time—and who would not feel himself obliged to do so. The human mind can never agitate gravely and earnestly, and according to the exigencies of its guilty condition, while unreconciled to God, the question of its eternal interests, but that its vices will be up, and prominent, and quick for mischief. And shall sinners, therefore, be permitted to sleep on, and go down to hell in their sins, because if they are awakened, some will behave themselves badly ?

The ostensible phenomena of revivals of religion in the United States, have exhibited themselves very much according to the characters of the communities affected, and of the individuals to whom, in the providence of God, have been committed the guidance and control of public feeling. In New England the character of the communities has always been of a grave and sober cast, where thought takes lead of feeling; and the temperament of the ministry more severe than ardent—more prone to stock the understanding than excite the passions. Hence the public excitements of revivals have never exposed the people or the ministers to extravagancies. The most remarkable characteristic of such seasons, is not noise but stillness—the reign of contemplative silence and solemn reflection. The world itself seems hushed, as if awed by eternity. The public assemblies are thronged, indeed, but the ordinary restive listlessness of an unthinking crowd is settled into a rapt attention of the soul, and into the silent, but not less expressive demonstrations of the deepest emotions. Public order is not less, but more exact. A violation of it would be the more shocking. There is no want of feeling, and no difficulty in controlling it. And I have yet to learn the occurrence of any notable disorders in all the revivals of New England, that have ever come to my knowledge. They may have happened, but I never heard even of one.

All is decency, and all quietness—not, however, the quietness of stupor, but of subdued feeling. A large portion of New England is literally educated to revivals. The present generation of ministers and churches has been born in them, and brought up in them, and is familiar with all their scenes. They understand the symptoms—they know what to do and how to do— and the people know how to behave. In the highest excitement of public feeling, it would be morally impossible to drive the people into disorder, or extravagance. They have no such habit. Such is the fixedness of their character, that no power on earth could essentially discompose the public mind.

But all this cannot be said of every portion of the population of our country. The farther West one goes, the less will he find of the stubbornness of a well-defined and fixed character, as the settlements are new, and society comparatively heterogeneous and unorganized. The farther South, — the more ardent and more excitable the people. But the medium of these extremes is of a character qualified between the two—I mean that medium of society, which is found in the intermediate territories.

And there are many, very many communities without, and some of them far without New England, in the states of New York, New Jersey, and Ohio, where revivals of religion are characterised with as much sobriety, as in the land of the pilgrim fathers. Irregularities and extravagance are no more essential attributes of revivals, than are the physical conditions of the territory and climate. They are mere accidents, when they happen to occur, owing to the state of society, or to the want of a proper superintendence, or to the combined influence of both these causes. A proper superintendence may at all times, and in any community, prevent them.

And, it may be asked, in what Christian country are not extravagancies in religion to be found ? Are they not to be found all over England, and Scotland, and Ireland ? Are they not to be found in the city of London ? Did it become me to say it, I would venture to affirm, and pledge myself to the proof, that there is not a state in Europe, where are not to be found more fanaticism, and more religious extravagance, in proportion to the population, than in the United States of America.

Take, for instance, the following notice of an

order, just issued from the War Department of
the French government, and deduce fairly what
it proves :—' The minister of war has addressed
a circular to all the general officers of the army,
directing them to warn the soldiers under their
command, against listening to the doctrines of
the *St. Simonians*, who openly propose the abolition of all individual rights in property, which
they wish to be intrusted to the chiefs of their
own sect, to be employed for the general good.
The minister directs, that reports be made to
him, as to such officers and men, as may appear
to yield to the seductions of these sectarians.'—
(*French Paper.*) What ! such a religious extravagance, attained such an ascendency in irreligious France, as to endanger the interests of the
army !—and require such an order !—nor is it
noticed as a very extraordinary thing.

Admit, there are real and substantial evils, incidental to revivals of religion, as doubtless there
are. What then?—Does it prove they are not
of God ? and no blessing to the world ? Suppose we should admit St. Paul's first epistle to
the Corinthians,—which had occasion to speak
of evils grown up in the Corinthian church, and
to apply a correcting hand to them,—as evi-

dence and conclusive proof, that Paul had lost his labour there, and that the Spirit of God had nothing to do in the establishment of that church. And suppose we should call his second epistle to the same community a chapter of flatteries, and an artful device to smooth over the difficulties, and to conceal his disappointments. Suppose we take all the candid acknowledgments of the Bible, from beginning to end, of the sins and imperfections of God's people, and of the difficulties and trials which prophets and apostles experienced in superintending them—and add to these the faults of prophets and apostles themselves—as so many proofs, and full proofs, that religion is nothing, and the church nothing, and Christianity nothing, but a thing got up of men. Suppose we set aside our discrimination, and surrender our imaginations to the long and pregnant chapter of scandal, which attaches to the church, in all the ages of its history, before and since the coming of Messiah, for its real imperfections. Suppose we take the most self-complacent portions of the church of our own day, and look only at the scandal that can be found there. Suppose we take the testimony of an unbelieving, slanderous, and opposing world, and abide by their opinion of the real value of religion, and of Christianity. All this would be as reasonable and as just, as to decide upon the merits of revivals of religion by their incidental evils,—as to listen to the slanderous and malicious reports of them. Did ever a genuine reformation of religion, in the hands of prophets, or apostles, or whatever men of God, in whatever age or part of the world, escape an evil report ?—Does Christianity, in the abstract, with all its immaculate purity, stand up before the world unimpugned ?

CHAPTER IX.

No man can be a good statesman, without a
minute acquaintance with the past history and
present state of the world. And he must be a
philosopher, too, in his discernment and estimation of moral causes, and tendencies, and probabilities, as they exist and are demonstrated in
human society. It is only by these qualifications, in highest perfection, and by the most skilful and vigorous application of them, on the
largest scale, that one nation can best secure its
own vantage-ground in relation to others. Such
are the policies of this world. ' And the children of this world are wiser in their generation,
than the children of light.' ' Ye can discern
the face of the sky—and can ye not discern
the signs of the times ?'

As statesmen, so Christians must work at great
disadvantage through ignorance. And I hope
to escape the accusation of arrogance, by the
reasons I shall offer, when I say :—That the

Christian world of the present day labours very extensively under all the disadvantage (and that is immense) of ignorance on a capital item of practical importance. And, that is,—*that the public opinion of the world, in the providence of God, is settled, immovably settled, in favour of Christianity.* I do not mean that well-informed Christians have not perceived this. Although it is probably a fact with many of them, that this truth has not yet burst upon them with all its light, and with all its animating influence. The habit of sympathizing with prophets and apostles, and primitive Christians, in all their trials, as well as in all their joys, as expressed and recorded on the pages of revelation; and the deference we pay to all the truths of the Bible, moral or historical, very naturally, and almost unavoidably, disqualify Christians of the present age for such classification of truths, as to enable them always to perceive,—that although moral truths are the same now as in the days of the apostles, always the same, yet general historical truths are not always the same.

It was a general historical truth in the days of Paul, that ' if any man will live godly in Christ Jesus, he shall suffer persecution.' But this is not, of course, true in all ages and in all countries. It was a general historical truth in the days of our Saviour, and seems to be so yet, ' that strait is the gate and narrow is the way that leadeth unto life, *and few there be that find it.* And wide is the gate and broad is the way, that leadeth to destruction, *and many there be that go in thereat.*' But this will not be true in the days of the Millennium. It was a general historical truth in the apostolic age (it might be difficult to say, in how many subsequent ages) that the public opinion of the world was against Christianity. But it is not so now. And yet the great bulk of the Christian world are ignorant of this fact. They read the Bible, have learned to sympathize with the first Christians, and imagine that, because the world were generally opposed to Christianity then, they are so still. They read church history, and sympathize with the martyrs of the *ten* great persecutions, and with the martyrs of a later time, and although they are not called to martyrdom themselves, they think the temper of the world is the same, but only modified in form *. You hear it

---

* Which is doubtless true in the evangelical sense. But I am now speaking of the temper of the world in the common sense of *public opinion.*

in their prayers—you hear it from the pulpit —it groans out from the press—it is uttered from every quarter of a suffering, agonizing church. And some, not a few, go so far as to imagine, that the darkest time the church has ever seen, is just about to come.

Now it is a pity that Christians, who have enough, in any case, to care for, should 'borrow trouble'—that they should waste their anxieties on false deductions. For every item of care, that is bestowed unnecessarily, is so much waste; —and not only so, but it fills a mind which ought to be occupied in doing positive good. Every prayer and every labour, spent against a mere imaginary danger, are all lost, and worse than lost. It is worse than ending at the place where we should begin, because the mind is unfitted to go on where alone it can be usefully employed. And here is the great, the immense disadvantage, under which many, perhaps the great majority of Christians of the present day, labour,—not appreciating the character of the age, 'not discerning the signs of the times.' It is unnecessary to write another book, or make another argument, or preach another sermon, to establish the supremacy of Christianity in the respect of mankind. That work is done, and done for ever. Not that there may not be some *local* occasions for efforts of this kind, and a continued demonstration of achievements already made. But I am speaking of the *grand* impression, as a whole, and as being decisive of the great question before the world. Christians now have only to take advantage of that impression—of that state of society, which God in his providence has induced, in the progress of 1800 years,—I might say, in the march of his providence since creation,—but more especially by the political and moral revolutions of eighteen centuries, all having a relation and tendency to this grand result;—they (Christians) have only to plant their feet upon this ground, start from this point, and, by one united and vigorous onset, march directly to the conquest of the world, in the use of the simple and naked weapons of evangelical truth.

If there be anything in this lower creation, with which men have to do, and which has to do with men, and yet too ghostly to be made the subject of a definition, it is *public opinion.* Though we cannot tell what it is, no one doubts its existence;—though it does not present itself in palpable forms, all men feel it. Its secret and invisible influence operates on every mind, and modifies every one's conduct. It has ubiquity, and a species of omniscience; and there is no power on earth so stern in its character, so steady, so energetic, so irresistible in its sway. Every other power must do homage at its altar, and ask leave to be. The thrones of kings stand by its permission, and fall at its beck. It is a power that lives, while men die,— and builds and fortifies its entrenchments on the graves of the generations of this world. With every substantial improvement of society, itself improves;—with every advancement of society, itself plants its station there, and builds upon it, and never yields. Time and the revolutions of this world are alike and equally its auxiliaries, and contribute by their influence to its maturity and increasing vigour. And this is the power, which has adopted Christianity, and set itself up its advocate and defender, in the hands of an Almighty Providence.

In the days of the apostles, and in subsequent ages, the public opinion of the world stood marshalled against Christianity. And it was not until after the political and moral convulsions of eighteen centuries—convulsions, in the bosom of which Christianity has been making its bed and planting its seeds:—it was not, until Spiritual Babylon had thoroughly disgusted and astounded the world by her arrogance and abominations;—it was not until the Sun of the Reformation, rolling on to the West, had gone down in that region where first he rose, and opened again his morning twilight on Luther's grave;—it was not, until infidelity had done its worst, 'and played such tricks before high heaven, as made the angels weep;'—it was not until Mohammedism and Paganism had wearied out the patience, and drank the very life-blood of the most enduring hope of man, and man had tried every possible expedient to work out his own redemption, but the only true one; —it was not, until every human and every diabolical invention, to overthrow the foundations and defeat the designs of Christianity, had been exhausted — Christianity in the meantime and all the while gradually settling down and gaining a stronger hold on the affections of mankind; —it was not, until all these grand events, and all that is comprehended in them, had transpired in the providence of God, that the world seems

H

to have consented, evidently consented, that Christianity should reign. And here is the point, at which the enterprise of Christians of these times may safely begin. This is the ground, which they ought to assume, as all cleared and settled at their hands.

It is true, indeed, that the human heart is the same as ever;—that man individually is the same;—that the entrenchments of idolatry and superstition on Pagan ground are yet widespread, and lofty, and formidable;—that Mohammedism is still a mighty power;—that Popery is yet strong;—that infidelity is abroad in the earth, and bold, and rampant;—that licentiousness raves to be freed from restraint, and to desolate society;—that thrones are tottering and kingdoms shaking, and men's hearts failing them for fear of what shall come;—and that the true Church, the last and only hope of the world, is rent by division, and more or less eagerly absorbed in controversy with the dissenting members of her own house;—the last, indeed, the worst of all.

But no matter for all this;—excepting only the dissensions of the house of God—and they are greatly less in number, and less virulent, than they were, and are diminishing every day. It is still true, that Christianity is securely established in the respect of the world. The world has found, that it cannot do without Christianity. However the Church may be divided, they all hold to the same creed—the Bible. However Christian nations may conflict with each other, they all hold to a common religion. And that religion pervades all the moral elements of their society, sanctifies everything that is good, confirms the civil, and hallows the domestic relations, and forces all men to feel their dependence upon its grace, and sanctions, and authority, for the security of all that is dear on earth. The very perversions, and abuses, and corruptions of Christianity, and that terrible revulsion of the human mind, which those corruptions have begotten and forced into being, infidelity in its worst shapes, have all and only contributed to make men feel the importance of true Christianity, and to dispose them to aid in its confirmation and establishment, as the basis and soul and crown of human society. The insolent pretensions and impudent scoffs of infidelity, and the mad ravings of licentiousness are little to be regarded, as an occasion of fear. They can gain no ascendency, except in the brief triumphs of a mob. At the same time, the steady march of the more stable institutions of society is onward, settling deeper and firmer on the foundations of Christian principle. Any truly Christian purpose, any purely Christian enterprise, may find a patronage and support in all Christian nations, among all ranks, and from all sects. Christian nations are alike disgusted with the arrogance of Papal Rome, as they are afraid of infidelity. They want true religion, and will never be satisfied without it. If there be a nation in Europe likely ever to renounce Christianity, few would hesitate in saying, that nation is France: yet with all their levity, and with all their irreligion, I cannot imagine there is any danger of it. The records of 1793 must be stricken from their history, before they could be persuaded to such a mad and desperate plunge *.

It is settled, then, that with Christian nations, Christianity is their only hope. All their more hallowed affections, seeking repose, hover round and light upon her altars, as a common sanc-

* The present extraordinary demand for the Bible in that country, is an omen of other promise, than the abolition of Christianity.

tuary. Their regard for its institutions is not diminishing, but increasing—it is fixed and settled for ever. They have learned to distinguish between the abuses of religion and its legitimate designs, and henceforth will seek to disencumber themselves of the former, and avail themselves of the advantages of the latter. And I need not say, that Christian nations are, in all respects, at the summit tide of influence over human affairs;—nor need I construct an argument to prove, that Paganism will melt away before Christianity, as snow and ice before the approach of a torrid sun, when once the splendour of its rays is made to blaze upon those regions of night, by the combined enterprise of Christian communities. Mohammedism and Popery will be the last to yield, and the world is already tired of both *.

Let Christians, then, assume the ground—that the public opinion of the world is settled—immovably settled in favour of Christianity, so far as the choice of religions is concerned. And the world will never try to do without religion. And the next step is, for true Christians to unite in applying all possible force to incorporate one

---

* I do not mean the last in order of time—for I pretend not to prophecy—but most stubborn.

other element with that opinion, *viz.*—the necessity of experimental religion, or a conversion of the heart to God, by the special agency of the Holy Ghost. And this, too, can be done, because, in the first place, it is a doctrine of the received and acknowledged text-book, the Bible. And next, because it is reasonable, and men are reasonable beings, and may be convinced in favourable circumstances. Public opinion advances slow and with difficulty; but when once organized, it is mighty—invincible.

And next and last, as the capital and crowning attribute of public sentiment, let the doctrine of *revivals,* in their true and proper sense, be promulgated and infused, and become a component element of common belief, throughout the Christian world—and then may a nation be born in a day. I cannot submit to the accusation of dreaming here. It is all practicable. It is in the line of Christian doctrine,—it is the highway of common sense,—it is the suggestion of experience. What is possible for a small community, is possible for a larger, is possible for the world, if it be founded in human nature, and accordant with the purpose of God. It is equally possible for the world to be established in the belief of revivals, as of Christianity, and easier. For having embraced the whole, they have embraced its parts;—having received the greater, they have comprehended the less. It is only necessary, that it should be made palpable by analysis, and a fair presentation. As the necessity and excellence of Christianity have been enforced upon the world by actual experiment, the same process is capable of confirming the world in the importance and necessity of revivals of religion, for the full accomplishment of the designs of Christianity. And the sooner the better. Let Christians be united in this enterprise. Let them be persuaded of the doctrine, and desire and strive earnestly to give revivals a full proof before the world. It is with them instrumentally to make the impression, and to form public opinion, in relation to the grand expedients of converting the world.

I hope I shall not be misapprehended by any person, as to what I mean by the public opinion of the world in favour of Christianity. It cannot, I think, be supposed I mean to assert that the world has thoroughly embraced Christianity; but rather, that Christianity, in the providence of God, has obtained such an estimation and such credit in those parts of the world, which may reasonably be supposed to have in their control the destinies of all mankind, as to be able to maintain its ground; that the cardinal principles of the morality and theology of Christianity have become so incorporated with the controlling influences of society, that they cannot henceforward be eradicated—cannot retrograde in their influence, but must advance with the advancements of society. I mean, that Christianity is in public, in general, in popular favour—in a favour, gained by so much time, and under so many revolutions of human society, that its tendencies and future results may fairly be considered matters of certain calculation, from the known attributes of human nature in the social state. And all this may be, and is in fact, a very different thing from a thorough and sanctifying operation of Christian principles to the same extent. It is great progress—but it is not the goal. It is a stage, an important and interesting stage, of the progress of Christianity towards a final conquest of the world. It has secured public opinion beyond the danger of being lost. It has no occasion to spend another effort for that object. This is precisely the point, where every power may and should be applied to a direct and vigorous onset for the immediate and thorough conversion of the world. The world will not only endure, but will welcome all and any efforts, which the precepts and spirit of Christianity require, or suggest. And this, certainly, must be allowed to be a cheering prospect for the church. Do Christians generally appreciate this state of the world? Do they understand the ' signs of the times'—the character of the age?—If this be well and thoroughly understood, I have not perceived it. There is evidently an indistinct perception of this kind, prevailing. But it does not seem to be well defined. Christians have talked long and much of the peculiar character of the age. But do they understand precisely the ground, on which they stand?

I am aware that one appears to disadvantage in seeming to be wise. And I have felt a reluctance to make these observations on that account. But it seems to be a very common license for every one to speak his own thoughts. And I hope it is not too early to advance such notions, as these. As I fully believe they are

justified by events, I must dare to risk them.
And I wish to be believed, that I do it from
humility, rather than arrogance. One thing I
will presume :—that if this assumption be a mistake, it is on the safe side—that it is eminently
practical—and if the whole Christian world,
from this moment, were to take this ground,
and act fully on this principle, they would be
likely to induce such a state of things, if it has
not already come ;—and if it has indeed come,
they would march directly to immediate and
certain triumph. Of course, whoever adopts
this belief is likely to do a greater amount of
good. The hope of success is the mainspring
of human enterprise.

This notion may indeed contradict some current interpretations of prophecy—or interpretations, which have been current. But by this
time, it seems to be allowed, that ' no prophecy
is its own interpreter.' Interpreters have unfor-
tunately for themselves in some instances set up
for prophets, and of course have entirely failed.
In attempting to expound the inspired visions
of prophecy, in application to the future grand
events of the world, they have proved themselves uninspired dreamers, and are now of

little authority *. Facts and common sense are more likely to be regarded, than the most ingenious interpretation of prophecy, which the pages of modern literature have spread out before us. Whoever may preach to the contrary, it will still be believed, because it is known and felt—that there is no character on earth in such general and high credit, as the purest Christian character. Wherever it is exemplified, the whole world, Christians and infidels, religious and irreligious, involuntarily approve it. It commends itself to the consciences of the most wicked and most abandoned. The Gallios, and the worldly-minded, and the most flagitious, all agree in this. And the only fault they have to find is—that professing Christians do not demonstrate it—do not live up to their professions. And this, I aver, is a true expression—a fair index of the public opinion of the world. The time has come, when Christians may do as much as they please, and all that they please, every thing possible, for their Divine Master; if they will only do it in

* I would not be thought to speak to the discredit of those students of prophecy, whose highly creditable investigations have thrown so much light and interest around this important portion of the sacred volume

the spirit of their Master, and the world will applaud and say, ' Now you act consistently.' Christianity has been long enough in the world for every body, in Christian lands, to know generally what its precepts enjoin, and that the fruits of obedience to its precepts are good. And their principal complaint is—that Christians do not do their own proper work fast enough. What an amazing advantage is this !—What power put into the hands of Christians ! Were all baptized Christians, Christians indeed —such Christians as the opinion of the world demands them to be, they would convert the world, and the whole world, in a very brief period ! The world lies at their feet, and seems to solicit them :—' Come and convert us !'

———————

CHAPTER X.

I CANNOT honestly propound myself, as thoroughly qualified to make a decision of the first of these two questions. The reason may be obvious: I am too ignorant of the particular history of religion in other parts of the world. And yet, perhaps, I may present considerations, which will enable observant Christians, in a country foreign to my own, to decide the question, as far as relates to themselves,—a tleast to decide on the probabilities. It is possible this object has already been attained.

I have endeavoured in former chapters, and generally, to convey my own distinct impression of the commencement of a series of Providential dispensations, in the United States, about one hundred years ago, of an extraordinary character, which are now generally known under the name of *revivals of religion*. I have in various forms attempted to define and fix the character of these dispensations, according to their phenomena—intimating, that the phrase, *revivals of religion,* in its ordinary grammatical and constructive sense, neither fully comprehends, nor exactly suggests the real character of the events, to which it is applied. And if I have not before fully educed the thought, it is essential to my present purpose, that I should here distinctly announce it (as a matter of opinion, of course)—that I have felt obliged to conclude, that this precise character of Divine dispensations was the commencement of a new era of Providence, in some of its forms, and when taken in its full and complete developement.

And now it will be considered incumbent upon me to make out the case. As I have merely hazarded an opinion, and am not conscious of any special zeal to maintain it, I shall not therefore attempt any elaborate argument. So far, indeed, as I may be supposed to desire a respect for my own judgment, I would not willingly make such a commitment of myself rashly. But I consider myself necessarily driven to this conclusion, and obliged to abide by it, merely as a philosopher, until I shall see sufficient reasons for changing that opinion.

For American revivals are *facts*, apparently out of the common order.

I assume, that it was the purpose of God, as revealed by his prophets, to open and to characterise the Christian dispensation generally and throughout, with some special effusions of his Holy Spirit, and that the speciality of this work began to display itself on the day of Pentecost —that it was largely demonstrated under the ministry of the Apostles—that it did not cease with the expiration of their labours—that ' at sundry times and in divers manners' this work has been sustained from the first age of Christianity to the present—that God has been all along and is now preparing the world for the more effectual and thorough operations of his Spirit,—and finally, that when the necessary revolutions of human society shall have been gone through, God will take the world by surprise, and convert the nations and people by his Spirit, through the truth, with a rapidity and power, not now easily to be credited.

It is matter of history, that for a century past, certain portions of the American Churches, or certain portions of the people, among whom those churches have been planted, have been visited with a remarkable influence—that that influence, in its precise and identical character, has been uninterrupted in the mean time—that for a few years now past, it has been spreading wider and increasing in its power—and that at the present moment it is displaying itself by diffusion and with an energy, before altogether unknown. We believe, that this is the work of the Holy Spirit of God. We have no reason to doubt it. There is no philosophy within the reach of man, that can otherwise account for it. I have expressed my opinion, that this work, in its entire developement, makes a new era of Providence—or to vary its form—a new and separate chapter of the Christian dispensation.

It is altogether unlike the former parts of the history of religion in the same country, upon the same premises, and among the same people, who were planted there more than two hundred years ago, and gradually grew up into import- ance to the time of the beginning of this period. They were a people, in the most rigid sense, and in the most prominent attributes of their character, strictly religious. And their religion was of a kind, eminently pure, elevated, and practical. They left Europe for conscience' sake, and founded in those regions a sort of religious empire — incorporating religion with the whole social fabric. And they maintained it, from generation to generation, with most scrupulous fidelity and watchful care. But it does not appear, that they were ever visited by this remarkable influence, till the time to which we have alluded—certainly not to any considerable extent—not enough to be a subject of special historical notice—probably not at all. I think it fair to conclude so.

And now where else shall we find its exact type? A *likeness* we can find. But the peculiar character of these dispensations is to be kept in view. It is not a forced religious attention. It is not simply a general attention to religion occasioned by a concentration of a special and extraordinary amount of instrumental and social influence. It does not consist of the multiplication of insulated conversions—which I have known to be without the occurrence of a proper revival. But it is the prevalence of an unseen influence, which seems to charge the whole moral atmosphere of a community at once and thoroughly with a deep religious solemnity, —which arrests the common current of this world's cares, and gives a bias of the popular mind to eternal things—which circulates with the rapidity of lightning through the ordinary channels of human sympathy,—and collects around the altars of the sanctuary, and bows down before the cross of the Saviour, in one company, multitudes of the rich and poor, the old and young, the man of pleasure and the man of business, every grade and condition of society. In one week, often in a day or two, a whole community may be seen, equally to their own surprise, as to that of all the world, transformed from a most worldly and reckless condition of the popular mind, to such deep and absorbing thoughts of eternal scenes. It may be either more or less striking than this description, according to the energy and extent of the influence bestowed—bestowed as we ought to allow from above. It is not the eloquence of man. It is God that speaketh—it is God that is heard—it is God that is felt. A George Whitfield might pass along, and draw the world around him, and make a deep impression; and sinners, here and there, might be converted through his instrumentality. But the moment he is gone, the religious atmosphere goes with him. Not so in a genuine revival of religion. It came not of man, and is dependant on no accident of this sort. Instruments, to be sure, may help or hinder it, may beautify or mar it, may render it as the garden of God, or disfigure it, and sow tares, and plant much evil fruit. These accidents may and do affect the work, but they do not annihilate its peculiar character.

Such as I have here and elsewhere described, though very imperfectly, is the character of American revivals of religion, having displayed themselves under the same identical forms for one hundred years. And the question now before us, is, whether these forms and this character of religious influence on the popular mind have been found in other ages and in other parts of the world? It has already been remarked, that they were not observable during the first hundred years of the colonial settlements of North America. And considering the character and habits of the people, so scrupulously exact in all religious observances, so conscientious, so thoroughly trained in the fear of God, we can assign no reason for the withholding of these extraordinary visitations, except by a reference to divine sovereignty. So it pleased God. And if we please, we can imagine a reason, why they should come when they did—a reason, which, in my own view, is worthy of great respect.

Suppose, then, that the designs of Providence in planting these colonies were to make a new and more advantageous experiment of human society, in its simplest and purest forms, by the hands of the purest and most devoted spirits— in regions remote from the older and more vicious institutions of civilized man;—that God intended there to give an example to all the world, not only of the practicability and supe-rior excellence of a popular government, but at the same time, being on the eve of introducing the Millennial period of his church, he intended also upon that ground to institute and exem-plify an extraordinary series of the outpourings of his Holy Spirit, in a state of society, such as before in all respects had never existed, and more, perhaps, than any other, favourable to the social and all-pervading influence of religion ;— and that God had resolved by such an influence and by such dispensations, not only to save that growing and wide-spreading community from the common wreck of the nations and kingdoms of this world, but to infuse into his Church

there an unwonted purity and energy, and thus
giving it in charge a leading influence, in company with other portions of his own elect, in the
career of evangelizing the world, and reducing it
to the empire of his anointed Son. On the
basis of this supposition, a light is shed upon
the path of God's actual providence. We can
seem to see why God should begin this work
where and *when* he did. It was not the common virtue of that people, that could save them
—virtuous as they may be allowed to have been.
As with all other communities and nations of
the earth, having the common elements of human depravity in them, the pride of prosperity,
the accumulation of wealth, and a never-satisfied
ambition, private and public, would necessarily
engender private and public corruption—and
corruption would lead on to convulsions, and to
the ultimate dissolution of the proudest empire,
which may yet be supposed to await them.
Nothing but some such extraordinary interposi-
tion of Providence, as that which is now under
consideration, instituted, and sustained, and carried on, and made to prevail, could ultimately
save even that people, in their most favourable
circumstances, from the common fate of the

nations of this world. Nothing but some such
interference could sustain a church, and purify
and enlarge it, and render it energetic in its
influence on the public mind, among a people,
where every man is his own lord, and walks at
large with none on earth to control him.
Nothing, apparently, but some such influence,
to be begun and to reign in some part of the
world, and to extend itself, could prepare the
way of the Lord, and usher in the latter day of
glory. And when, it may be asked, was a
better time, and where more favourable circumstances ?

Just at the moment, when that community
began to develope its own gigantic powers, to
anticipate its own destiny, and to aspire after
national importance, this work of God also began
to exercise its qualifying and redeeming powers.
And now, that that community has actually
come to the full stature of manhood, and attained a proud summit of national greatness,
this same work of God has gone through an
experiment of one hundred years, suffered the
worst reverses, to which such an extraordinary
series of dispensations may be supposed to be
liable in the hands of imperfect men, has gained

all the advantages of such a long course of experience, and is now in the full tide of a successful and triumphant career. So much for the reasons, why these events were to be expected, and why they were necessary. And if this be called a theory, it cannot certainly be stigmatized with the name of a mere hypothesis. For it is sustained by the indications of Divine prophecy, by the most reasonable presumptions growing out of the revealed economy of God,— and what is more, it is sustained by facts. It is formed out of facts, and built upon them.

And this same class of reasons may naturally suggest the thought, that there are probably some *peculiarities* in American revivals of religion. The Spirit of God seems to have exerted a more manifest and mighty energy there, than is ordinarily observed in other portions of the church, in these latter days. So I infer, from all the information I have been able to collect— and more especially from the surprise and incredulity, which are shown in other parts of the Christian world, in relation to this work of God in the United States. This surprise, though an indirect evidence, has seemed to me a very conclusive one. The history of religion in England seems to afford examples of many considerable religious excitements. But I am 'not able to satisfy myself, whether any of them are precisely of the same character with what I esteem the most genuine American revivals. And from the want of general respect and good estimation, which many of these religious excitements on this side of the Atlantic have suffered, even with good men, I feel obliged to suspend my judgment concerning them. I have been forced to notice, that American revivals have suffered in England not a little, by a comparison with what has been exemplified in religious excitements here. All which serves to convince me, that there must be some radical differences between the two.

The energy of God's Spirit in the days of the apostles was certainly very remarkable, — and the day of Pentecost was doubtless the most remarkable of all, not reckoning the miracle of tongues. But I think it fair to conclude, that the state of society in any part of the Jewish, or Roman, or Grecian world, could not afford the most advantageous combination and relative position of the moral elements in the social states, for the operation of religious influences,

through the medium of human sympathy. But
it pleased God, in the first setting up of Christianity, to bestow an amount of grace and an
energy of influence, which to a great extent
triumphed over these disadvantages, and made a
thorough and an everlasting impression on the
world. It was expedient, and doubtless necessary, that it should be so. The first age of
Christianity was in all respects extraordinary.
And we cannot compare it with any other, nor
any other with it, expecting to find an exact likeness. And without instituting any other points
of comparison with the first age, the present, all
other things being equal, is far more favourable
for the energetic and thorough operation of Christianity, and is every year becoming more and
more so. The conditions and aspects of human
society are entirely changed—changed to an
extent, that can hardly be conceived. And I
hope I shall not be accused of any undue national partialities (for it is impossible to do
justice to this theme, without being unrestrained
by such an apprehension—I hope, therefore, to
be appreciated) when I say, that the history of
the world, since the introduction of Christianity,
does not probably afford, in any of those re-

gions which Christianity has visited—nor any-where else, so far as I know,—a state of society more felicitously combined, in the relations of life, for a quick and thorough operation of the social and sympathetic influence of religion, through the entire community, than the United States of America. Observe, I say—through the *entire* community. Any particular *grade* of society in any country always has a more perfect sympathy, other things being equal.

So far, however, as the general state of society is advantageous, or otherwise, for the circulation of religious influence, it is doubtless more the character of the age, of the present period of the world (I speak of the Christian world generally), than of any particular community. One community may indeed have this character in a higher degree—in a condition more susceptible, taking into consideration the relations of all its parts and its general attributes;— but still it is rather the character of the age. The communities and nations of Christendom are not sufficiently disjunct, not to have very essentially a common sympathy on the great practical questions of morality and religion. The advancements of society in knowledge and in religion, and in other correlative improvements, are not so much in insulated conditions, as in a general current. Certain local accidents, by the existing operation of some peculiar institutions and relations of society, may indeed retard or hasten the developement of such improvements. But still the advancement of society in all the cardinal principles of virtue and religion, and of the social states, is in a measure common throughout the civilized world. The intercourse of mind cannot be restrained. It sympathises through countless and undefined channels, especially through that chief of all mediums, the medium of letters—that mighty engine of human improvement, the press. It is this, which breathes and circulates every valuable thought through the world, with the rapidity of electric influence. It may not be seen to operate, as soon as it is embraced and cherished. There may be hinderances. But still it is cherished, and takes root, and springs up, and ramifies, and will ultimately prevail. The march of society in all essential improvements, therefore, is a general current.

The temper of one community may happen to be easier in its susceptibilities; or the forms of its construction more favourable to the speedy developement of the treasures of its experience and observation ; or the impediments in the way of putting into immediate execution important and useful suggestions, may be less; or the combined influences of these several and other favourable causes, may together contribute to give a leading influence to one community, or nation, over another, in the march of improvement in this, that, or another particular; or in general. But still where the advantages of general literature, and of the periodical and daily press, are common,—where the press for all its purposes is free and unrestrained, and where commercial and social intercourse is open, and constant, and generous,— there is always a quick and simultaneous sympathy on all great subjects of human improvement, throughout the world. Whatever good thing is made evident in one place, is easily and soon transplanted to another.

So far, therefore, as there is any peculiarity in American revivals, admitting them to be the genuine fruit of the legitimate agencies of Christianity, it can only be regarded as an earlier, a more full, and more energetic developement, under the Spirit of God, of those favourable combinations of the moral elements of society, which are characteristic of the age. It is possible, and not improbable, that the facilities for the sympathetic influence of religion are greater and more general in the United States, than anywhere else, taking society as a whole. But although the grades of society there are not so distinct, and the barriers between them are not so impervious to a common sympathy, as in England, and in the nations of Europe; yet as a whole, it is not so much one, nor so truly sympathetic, as every separate grade in European communities, taken by itself.

In the United States society is altogether more heterogeneous, when it is considered as embracing the whole population, in comparison with a particular rank of any other community. And if there be any reason in philosophy, why religion should prevail through society there, as a whole, by such considerations; there is still more reason, why it should prevail here, in any grade, taken by itself, through the application of the proper means. Because a common sympathy within such limits, is altogether more perfect.

That the secret and peculiarities of American

revivals, so far as there are any, do not depend on the peculiar structure of society in that country, may be settled by a single historical consideration, which has before been adduced :—And that is, that these revivals were unknown till the original and constitutional elements of that community, in their distinctive peculiarities, had been in full operation for more than a hundred years, and under circumstances, in human view, altogether more favourable for such results, so far as they may be supposed to depend on such attributes.

Indeed, revivals of religion, such as I have intended to define them, are acts or visitations of Divine sovereignty, and have no such connexion with the common philosophy of ethics, as to enable us to point out any possible given things in society, or in the power of man, with which they are certainly and of course to be connected. Philosophy, perhaps, may teach us in what particular structure of society they are likely to prove most thorough and energetic. But it cannot teach us where they may certainly be expected. They are dispensations, which God has reserved in his own absolute sovereignty, and for which he will have his people feel their dependence. They are special out-pourings of the Spirit. We know very well, however, or ought to know, that it is a part of God's sovereignty to regard the desires of his people. And it is agreeable to fact, as I have shown in a former chapter, that in the United States, these extraordinary influences are actually dispensed on the instant, and in a degree, com-mensurate with the amount of desire and corre-sponding efforts for this specific object. Not that they are never dispensed, independent of this desire and these efforts. For I have also shown, that instances of the latter have appa-rently occurred. But we have reason enough, in the history of Providence, to assert, that there is always and invariably a connexion be-tween the faithfulness of God and the faith of his people, as well for this, as for other objects. And the facts, that they rest in Divine sovereignty, and the providential disclosure of this one con-dition of that sovereignty, ought to settle these two questions:—first, that they do not depend on the structure of society for the fact of their occurrence; and next, that, however they may be bestowed independent of faith, they never disappoint faith. That is, faith is sure to bring them.

Let not Christians anywhere imagine, that revivals of religion are so qualified by the structure of society, as too hastily to conclude, that they have them, so far as is possible to have them, in respect to their character. There is a marked and wide difference between a religious excitement, let it be ever so considerable, which produces only insulated conversions, and these special outpourings of the Spirit. It is possible, I imagine, for honest Christians, desirous of the largest public blessings of a religious nature— desirous of the special effusions of the Spirit —to think they have this blessing in fact, though less in degree, than what is desirable, when they have it not. But however those, who have never experienced revivals, may err in their conceptions of them, or be in doubt as to what constitutes them, there can be no doubt, where they have actually occurred. There is a power in them, and a communicative, or circulating power, acting upon so many minds, and in such forms, that observant Christians cannot be ignorant of the speciality of the influence. They will feel it themselves, and be constrained to say—' it is the Lord's hand, and marvellous in our eyes.' And when they are without the positive testimony of the fact before their eyes, and consequently without its influence acting upon their hearts, if they entertain respect for the testimony of fellow-Christians, who know by experience what such things are, they may be equally certified of the absence, as of the presence, of this remarkable influence.

Once more:—It ought not to be admitted, I think, for a moment, that the most desirable, most effectual, and most thoroughly-reforming agencies of Christianity, are dependent on any peculiar structure of society. These agencies are designed to renovate the world. And the world obviously must be taken as it is, exhibiting infinitely varied forms of the social states. Take the limited experiment of Christianity on the world during the age and under the ministry of the Apostles. And surely a greater variety, or more unfortunate structure of society probably never presented, or ever will present, than the wide and various field of the Christian triumphs of those days. And what was the power,

which gave to Christianity such energy then?—
With the Christian, there can be but one answer
to this question:—It was the power of the
Holy Ghost. And so long as the Acts and the
several Epistles of the Apostles are extant, as
authentic, Christian records, inspired and sealed
of God, a single doubt ought not to lurk in a
Christian's mind, that God is able by the power
of his Spirit to revive religion, and to revive it
under the greatest disadvantages of any structure and any condition of human society.

And more especially, if it is indeed true, that
the public opinion of the world is in favour of
Christianity, as I have endeavoured to show;—
if it is indeed true, that by the revolutions of
opinion, as well as of society, under the action
of Christianity for eighteen centuries, God, in
his providence, has brought the world to an
eventful crisis, and to a crisis more susceptible
of favourable change, as seems to be the common impression;—and if it is indeed true, that
the unbelieving world are actually brought to
such positions, as to stand waiting for the direct
and subduing influences of our holy religion;—
then I ask, is not this a cheering, animating prospect? Is not this the time to make one united,

vigorous, determined onset? And since it is obviously and equally true, to a considerable extent, (and this state of things growing more and more confirmed every year)—that Christians are gradually laying aside their sectarian feelings and sectarian weapons, and learning by experience how much better and how much pleasanter it is to unite for the conversion of the world—as in the grand missionary enterprises of the age (this single denomination being understood to comprehend all other forms of Christian benevolence); — since the Christian world are entering upon these enlarged schemes with an energy of purpose, and a freshness of expectation, evidently big with events, and cheering beyond all former example;—and since contemporaneously with this condition of the world and of the church, God has actually begun to pour out his Spirit in larger and more plentiful effusions, than the experience of former and darker ages records;—then I ask again, is it not reasonable, in view of all these facts, and of all these symptoms, to expect — ought not Christians to expect, a descent of the Holy Ghost upon all Christian lands, where the Church is pure and faithful, in a manner and to a degree commensurate with the exigencies of such an interesting and eventful state of the world?—I cannot believe—I cannot trust myself to believe—I have not so little charity, as to believe, that Christians, with the Bible in their hands, do not expect a general and universal revival of religion, by such outpourings of the Spirit, as the world has never seen—as the Church has never yet experienced. And can they be surprised—will they be afraid, when there is a cloud in the heavens no bigger than a man's hand?—And shall not this be the age—this the day—in their hopes, in their faith, in their prayers, in their labours, for such events?

————————————

CHAPTER XI

NOTWITHSTANDING it is to be believed, that the
public opinion of the world is settled in favour
of Christianity, yet this is a very different thing
from a cordial acceptance of its practical and
experimental truths—a very different thing from
a full submission to its authority. It is a sort
of passing complaisance, which cannot reasonably be withholden, and which after all is not
very cordially rendered. It is enforced by the
merits of the claim, and constantly gaining a
more powerful dominion, by a resignation of the
contest on the part of the ruling spirits of this
world, by their tacit and habitual deference, and
by an ostensible positive respect, more or less of
which is sincere, so long as religion does not
make too earnest a demand upon their hearts.
The world is actually hemmed in. It cannot
get out of the commitment and surrender, which
are made to Christianity. But observe : the

world is not subdued. The entrenchments of human depravity, of the principalities of this world, of spiritual wickedness in high places, and of the powers of darkness, are yet high and strong—not unshaken, but unreduced. They are, indeed, encompassed by besieging forces, which God has brought around them, and planted in close and thick and formidable array, and to whom he has promised victory. A correspondence has been opened, and articles of capitulation signed—all except *one:* the heart has not yielded. And this is the point to be gained—a great point —the last point—and which, when yielded, will make a thorough conquest of the world.

The ordinary march of Christianity, such as the world now generally exhibits, can hardly be called a march. There are constant accessions, indeed, to the visible Church, by insulated conversions; but the portals of the grave and eternity are as constantly open to admit the leading ranks of the Christian host. There is, indeed, a new spirit of brighter omen kindling up here and there, throughout the Christian world, and essaying enterprise upon a grander scale, than in former days—making great impressions on the heathen, as well as on the Christian world. But this is often quenched, in a measure, and always embarrassed and checked, partly by inherent personal defects of the individuals, who are quickened by its energies,—partly, and not a little, by a want of the most perfect fellowship of Christians, and the discouragements and obstacles which they throw in each other's way,—and greatly, most formidably, by all the opposing tendencies of the world. With all the advantages that have been gained, still Christianity labours, still the Church agonizes. As in the language of prophecy—the Church seems to have come to the birth, but is unable to bring forth.

And what Christian will deny, that in such circumstances, which I think must be sufficiently evident to all, some great and powerful impulse from on High, is wanting?—I ask Christians, who believe in the Bible—who *believe* in it *fully*—I ask them, what is the appropriate office of the Holy Ghost?—What do they mean by their prayers, when they ask for the Holy Ghost to be *poured out* on themselves, on the Church, on the world? Do they mean something—or do they mean nothing?—and how much do they mean?—How do they understand the abundant and multiform predictions of the word of God, announcing the *outpourings* of the Spirit in the latter days? Can they believe, that all this imagery has been grouped and made to bear on this single topic—and all this extraordinary language employed merely to raise expectation, and then disappoint it—to mock and tantalize hope?—to announce, not an extraordinary, but a common event?—And what do they think of the day of Pentecost, and other like scenes of primitive times?—And do they not feel, one and all, that something extraordinary of this kind is absolutely necessary to fulfil the designs of Christianity?—Are there any stores of their own experience and observation, adequate to produce a faith in their hearts, that this world can ever be reduced to the condition of submission to God, in the full sense, and to the extent of the requisitions of the Gospel, independent of the special and almighty agencies of the Holy Ghost?—Do they believe that the Holy Ghost is concerned in the conversion of a sinner, and of every sinner that is converted?—Do they believe it possible for the Holy Ghost to convert two sinners at one time?—and twenty?—a hundred?—a thousand?—a whole

community, as well as one individual?—And is
it not obvious, that conversions must proceed
upon a larger scale, than what is ordinarily experienced in these days, in order that the Church
may gain upon the world, with a prospect of
bringing all the world within her pale?—What
but the Holy Spirit can shake off the drowsiness,
and disperse the unbelief, and dissolve the inactivity of the professing people of God?—What
but the Holy Spirit can thoroughly awaken
sinners, and bring them to repentance, and
multiply converts unto Zion?—What but the
Holy Spirit can impart to Christians the full
light and power of faith, and the energy of
Christian enterprise?—What but the Holy
Spirit can effectually encounter and disperse the
rulers of the darkness of this world?—What
but this Almighty Power can act efficiently upon
the huge mass of the depraved and troublous.
elements of this world, which make it a scene
of constant strife and bloodshed—that it may become an empire ' of righteousness, and of peace,
and of joy in the Holy Ghost?' Is there a
Christian on earth, that believes this work can
be done too fast, or too soon?—And if it is to
be done soon—if it is to be done within the

limits of the most reasonable expectations created by Divine prophecy—must it not be done fast?

Here, then, I take my stand, confident of one thing:—that from all views of human nature and of human society, as the principles of each and both combined have actually been developed —from a retrospect of all former experiment of Christianity, in its action on the world—and by most reasonable constructions of the word of God; prophetic and doctrinal,—an order of dispensations, by the plenteous and extraordinary outpourings of the Holy Spirit, like that I have defined, as characterizing revivals of religion, is reasonably to be expected—is absolutely necessary for the final subjection of the world to Jesus Christ. Independent of the introduction and maintenance of such an order of Providence, and of its continuous carrying on with great and unremitted power among the nations of the earth, the march of Christianity apparently must rest—perhaps itself be overthrown. For great as are the advantages it has gained, the world was never made to stand still. That strong hold on public opinion, which is now the undoubted property of Christianity, if neglected, if not improved for the thorough subjugation of human hearts, will by and by be wasted—and the world will go back again—yes, backward into another night of pantheism. (Not of atheism —for man was never made to be an atheist—he cannot be an atheist, as a race—however individuals of the species may think for a while they are so.) But this, however, is all supposititious, involving a condition, the darkest result of which, I trust, does not await the destinies of our world. ' We have not so learned Christ.' Christianity has spread before us a brighter page. It is not incomplete, nor insufficient, in its apparatus of means and agencies. As there is a Son of God and a Saviour, so is there a Holy Ghost. As there is One who has shed his blood, so is there One to apply that blood. There is a power in store, waiting to be poured forth, the tokens of which we have already had —a power adequate to bring this world back to God. And independent of that power—independent of its more special and more mighty manifestations, in some such order as I have described, I confess, I see not for one, how this object can ever be accomplished.

And it is remarkable, that Christians unanimously profess to expect such events. It is found in their creeds—it is heard continually from the pulpit—it is always involved in their prayers. And when these events come, are they surprised?—When their prayers are answered, shall they be frightened?—When the Holy Ghost descends, will they run away, and say, we wanted no such thing?—Let themselves define what they do want—what they mean—what they expect:—if, indeed, they want nothing, mean nothing, expect nothing. If sinners are awakened, and 'come running in and fall down, saying, sirs, what shall we do to be saved?'—shall it be said of Christians and of Christian ministers, that they do not know what to do?—and if sinners are converted, that Christians think it strange?—If multitudes are awakened and multitudes converted, for which Christians offer up their prayers every day, shall it then be made manifest, that these prayers were mere hypocrisy?—Let Christians answer these questions before God, if there be any honesty in them. Or will they presume to prescribe the forms, in which the Holy Ghost shall appear, and decree that He shall appear in no other?—If this is after all the secret of their distrust, it is indeed a lamentable one. Can they make human nature other, than what it is ?—Or do they expect miracles?—Or, finally, do they wish to be excused alike from miracles, and from the operations of the Holy Ghost upon human nature, such as it is?

But perhaps it will be thought—I have somewhat digressed, in mixing this expostulation, with a showing of the prospects of revivals of religion for the world. But is there not some apology, when we are invaded at all points, by the infidelity of the Christian world upon this subject?—May God remove that infidelity, stop the mouths of gainsayers, and speedily convince the whole world, by the actual, and multiplied, and extensive effusions of his Spirit, that nothing else is adequate to the designs of Christianity—that there is no other prospect for the effectual redemption of the world from ignorance, and sin, and suffering!

The *experience* of the Church, in the religious excitements, or revivals of modern times, under the existence of the present and more favourable conditions of human society, is of great value, in estimating their prospective influence on the world. The results of great experiments on society, whether political, civil, or religious, and the suggestions which they afford, are public property, wherever they occur, so far as the history of them is known. Take, for instance, the history of American revivals : and all the experience which they afford, is the property of the Christian world, and may be made available to the common cause. And certainly it can hardly be considered of trifling importance. The churches and people of the United States, to a considerable extent, enough to influence the whole mass of the population, and ultimately, if not already, to control the public opinion of that wide community on this subject, have treasured up all the advantages of one hundred years' uninterrupted experience in revivals of religion—and such revivals, as I have endeavoured to define and depict in this volume. I cannot affirm, that these revivals are peculiar to the United States—although I have given some reasons to show why, in some respects, they probably are so. Nor can I affirm any other, than as a matter of opinion, that they are eminently the work and power of God—and that they are so many tokens of his Providence set up, not only to increase the faith, and animate the hopes, and multiply the energies of his people, and lead them on to greater and nobler enterprise,—but as a sign to signify, that God is coming to claim possession and empire of the earth for his Anointed Son. And yet I am strongly disposed to believe, that such is their character, and such not unlikely their design. And entertaining this opinion, (which I think may be allowed to be innocent, even though it should prove a mistake,) it is a very natural inference, that just so far as they are of this character, so far also is there a gain of experience to the Church, in this work of God. And that such experience is valuable and greatly important, is sufficiently evident from the fact, that it has taken one hundred years to outlive the disasters of inexperience, and to acquire a comparatively full tide of successful experiment, through the instrumentality of a host of disciplined advocates, who in the mean time have been training up, and are constantly accumulating in numbers and influence. Admitting that these events are the work of God, in the sense which I humbly presume to claim for them— admitting, that they are the coruscations and gleaming heralds of a better and brighter day, shooting across the heavens, to give hope and courage to a suffering and waiting Church ;— admitting also, that human instrumentality is an essential agent in the Divine economy for the renovation of the world—then is it manifest, that the wisdom of a century's experience in the management of revivals of religion, is no unimportant acquisition to the Church of God on earth.

Whether indeed this experience is alone the property of the American churches—or principally so, I cannot presume to say. When, however, Christians on this side the Atlantic, are generally gazing at reports of these events, wondering and doubting what they are, it seems to afford an indirect evidence, that the same things are not so often found here. Religious excitements there may be and have been, greater or less, all over the Christian world. And the Church is constantly augmented by insulated conversions. Drops of Divine influence are ever falling here and there, and softening and melting hearts under their touch.

But we are now speaking of *showers*—showers which *rain* down righteousness—which come *pouring* from the heavens—so that not a tree nor a shrub, nor the smallest spire of vegetation can escape its influence. Or to drop the figure—we are speaking of such outpourings of the Spirit of God upon communities, as that all shall feel it, and many shall be converted to God. And this is what I mean by revivals of religion. They are dispensations of Divine Providence, which in the United States are well known, because they have been long time and in many places experienced.

And there is another important advantage, resulting from revivals of religion, besides experience in promoting them, and in the instrumental guidance and control of the public mind, under these remarkable dispensations of Providence, so as to bring out of them the richest and the best fruits—and that is, an elevation of the standard of piety, and a great advance in the general improvement of Christian character. To be born again in such an atmosphere, leaves impressions never to be forgotten, and imparts an impulse to sanctified affection, to the holy passions of the souls, which endures, and gives a lasting and efficient energy to piety. It creates a spirit of self-denial, of self-devotion, and of self-sacrifice—a willingness and determination to encounter obstacles and to brave danger in the cause of Christ—to spend and be spent in his service. At the outset of the Christian course, it gives opportunity for the immersion of the whole soul in a state of feeling, which for the time seems to ' know nothing but Christ and him crucified.' He who is born into the kingdom at such a time, tastes the sweets of communion with God in a high and special degree, of a fellowship with saints to be esteemed above all price, and imbibes deeply of the Saviour's agony for a perishing world. He gets to feel, that there is nothing worth living for but Christ—nothing worth labouring for, but the conversion of sinners, and the salvation of souls. And Christians of older standing are recast into the same mould, and come out reanimated, and as if filled and actuated by a new spirit. There is a sensible and great improvement of the general character of the Church—of individual character—and a general impression, that higher attainments in piety, and greater exertions for the cause of Christ are imperatively demanded. And these are not only the objects of fervent aspiration and earnest pursuit, but to a great extent and in a multitude of instances, they are actually attained and demonstrated— and that as the fruit of the impulse of revivals.

When we inquire into the religious history of those devoted men and women, who have gone forth from the American churches, as missionaries to the heathen, we generally find, that the spirit of their enlarged and aspiring enterprise was cradled in a revival. If we see a man very distinguished for his activity and usefulness in the church, or notable for his energy and success in the ministry, we may expect to find, that this character in its origin and formation had some intimate connexion with revivals. If we inquire whence comes the great bulk of the contributions, in the United States, for the support of the grand benevolent enterprises of the age, larger and smaller, we may trace the streams upwards to those generous and perennial fountains, which have been opened and sanctified by revivals. And I think I am justified in saying, that all, that is most remarkable in the American Churches for elevation and fervor of piety, for determined, persevering, and successful Christian enterprise, has owed its origin to a baptism in the spirit of revivals.

But the probabilities of a *perpetual* revival of religion—a revival without a consequent decline—an outpouring of the Spirit not to be withdrawn, or relaxed, so as to bring in all of the same and of every community and every nation, and to support all in a steadily progressive course of sanctification—is altogether and infinitely the most interesting and most cheering prospect of this grand economy of God, which has been introduced into the world in these latter days.

It is a remarkable feature in the history of revivals, where they have occurred many times successively, in the same community, in the course of a number of years, that the first instance, other things being equal, always produces the greatest shock, or greatest convulsion of the public mind. By the very supposition, the dispensation being extraordinary, the moral elements of the particular community had been *unaccustomed* to such influences. The operation of the whole, therefore, in the first instance, especially if the work be powerful, is somewhat of the nature of a sudden and astounding surprise. The public mind is arrested unexpectedly, and seems brought to a solemn pause. This novel agitation of the moral elements, this unwonted stirring up of the deep fountains of feeling, in view of religious truth, takes all minds, of Christians as well as others, and often of ministers, by surprise. And unless there is some experience of such a state of things to guide and control the public feeling, there is danger of some degree of unhealthful excitement, of some irregularities, and in particular instances, of unhappy results. And notwithstanding the effect, as a whole, is greatly good, —notwithstanding many sinners are converted, the Church enlarged, Christian character improved, irreligion invaded and greatly reduced in its forces,—yet there are some incidental evils, resulting from inexperience and the common vices of human nature. These evils, however, are of little consideration, when weighed against the good ; yet desirable to be prevented, and, to a great extent, possible to be prevented by experience. These incidental, and, in consequence of inexperience, unavoidable evils, limit a revival in its duration, qualify the sobriety of its influence, and detract from the richness of its fruits.

The second revival in the same community is always more sober, even when equally powerful, —is ordinarily more protracted, richer in its good fruits, and accompanied with less unhappy results. The third and fourth, and every successive revival, increase the amount of experience in the church and with ministers, the general temper of the community becomes accustomed, popular opinion increases in favour of such dispensations, until by and by, and in many instances, scarcely a voice is ever raised, or a word muttered against them. They are habitually sought for, prayed for, and laboured for, by the Church; and they are very sure to come in answer to such prayers, and in reward of such labours. Where there has been one revival, there is more apt to be a second—and a second is still more apt to induce a third, and a third a fourth, and so on, till a Church and the community, in which it is planted, become disciplined to such a state of things,—and they all together approximate gradually to the condition of a perpetual revival. There comes to be so much piety in the Church, so much ardour of Christian feeling, so much faith, and so much labour, that instances of awakening and conversion become of habitual occurrence; and the Spirit seems continually hovering over such a community, ever and anon scattering here and there the drops of his influence, and occasionally pouring down upon them the showers of his grace. And the progress of such a state of things exhibits more and more the promise and

the earnests of a perpetual shower   I could
name many communities in the United States,
which have exhibited all these grades of advancement, in the experience of revivals of religion, and which seem approximating constantly
to the condition of that uninterrupted, unbroken
influence, which is likely to operate a thorough
purification.   And others are treading in their
steps.   And we may well suppose, that the
reasons, why a revival is not *one* and *uninter-*
rupted, are vested in the inexperience of Christians, and in the vices of instrumental management, which result from such inexperience.

The school of training to these extraordinary
outpourings of the Spirit, must evidently be
gone through, in every community, in every
nation, and in all the world, before they are
likely to be perpetual and thorough in their
purifying operation.   It is reasonable and philosophical, that it should be so, so long as God
ordains and resolves to employ human instrumentality for the accomplishment of his redeeming influence over the world.   And this simple
analysis of the actual and historical progress of
these dispensations, goes to awaken the hope and
to confirm the conviction, that the proper eco-

nomy of revivals of religion combines all the elementary influences, including those vested in man, and those vested in the Holy Spirit, the tendencies of which are directly and ultimately to bring about one equable, uninterrupted, ever-lasting, and holy revival. And is not this a prospect, in Christian hope, cheering beyond the power of language to express—beyond imagination fully to appreciate?—And is it not reasonable too?

———

CHAPTER XII.

IT is the province of philosophy generally to
ascertain the causes of existing facts, and the
modes of their operation. And under this definition, it is easy to see, that it belongs to religion,
as well as to anything else. The vulgar notion,
which has prevailed to some extent, that religion
is to be rescued from philosophical proof, is
entirely erroneous. Christianity does not assert
its claims without reason——nor without reasons
palpable to common observation. It has from
the beginning, and in all the grades of its pro-
mulgation, to the filling up of its canon of
ordinances, challenged investigation. And down
to the present time, it has endured with triumph
the severest tests, which those indifferent to its
interests, and its declared and accomplished

adversaries have been able to bring to bear upon it.

And not only does Christianity commend itself to the belief of man, as a system of religion, sustained by philosophical proof, in all the historical traces of its origin, and of its filling up, down to the seal of a Saviour's blood, which has been affixed to it, and to the last miracle of the apostles;—but the spiritual world, the affections of the mind, on which it is designed to operate for their purification, are equally within the scope of philosophical observation,—before, during, and after the change, which Christianity claims to produce. Indeed, it is impossible to find an adequate cause for the phenomena of mind, as exhibited under the influence of Christianity, but by a resort to one of its cardinal doctrines:—viz., the agency of the Holy Spirit. True philosophy adopts the best reasons, that can be found, for a fact, or a class of facts, forcing themselves upon observation. And hence it is truly philosophical and satisfactory to find, in the doctrines of Revelation, declared and specific reasons for the influence of its doctrines. More especially as a reason cannot be found anywhere else.

There is another branch of the philosophy of religion—somewhat nice indeed—but yet palpable to experience, and important to be observed—viz. : the ascertainment of the boundary between our own duty and the work of the Spirit. If the moral economy of Christianity is fixed and immutable in relation and in adaptation to the moral economy of human nature—as we have reason to suppose it is—then it is impossible, that Christianity should produce its intended and proper effect, except as the human mind is brought in immediate contact with its truths and agencies. Christianity and the soul of man must be paraded, front to front—must look each other in the face—and then, and not till then, will the conscience feel compunction, the feelings flow out in repentance, and the heart submit itself to God. They may be in the same neighbourhood, they may live together in the same family, they may be for years in company, and yet it is possible there should be little, or no common sympathy between them. And the reason—or the *philosophy* of it is—they are not brought together—they are not put in close contact. The mind is not forced to make acquaintance with itself, by opening its eyes on the direct rays of Divine truth. Or rather — those rays are not brought, by the proper ministrations, to such a direct bearing. Without a miracle, it is impossible, under such disadvantages, that sinners should be converted, or religion revived. The moral economy of Christianity, including the respective agencies of Divine truth and the Divine Spirit on the human heart, is fixed. And the moral economy of human nature is fixed. And both these economies are adapted to each other. That is:— the system and agencies of Christianity are adapted to repair human nature, when brought into a given relation to it ;—and human nature, in the same relation, is likely to be healed of its vices.

But to expect the conversion of sinners, or the revival of religion, without this relation and juxta-position of the apparatus of redemption to its object, is a vain confidence. In other words —there is *philosophy* in the instrumental adaptation of the means of Christianity to their intended purpose ;—or such things, as knowing and not knowing how to do it with skill and success. And this philosophy consists partly in a knowledge of the human heart, of the avenues

by which Divine truth enters there, and in
the tact of enforcing its entrance. Without
this skill of ministration, the use of Divine
truth is a bow drawn at a venture, which
may, indeed, occasionally hit. But the reason
of it in such cases is not understood. And are
we of course to presume, that this reason is altogether beyond our reach—beyond the appropriate field of our own observation?—There is
doubtless an action of mind here, and consequently mental phenomena, known to him who
is the subject, and capable of being disclosed to
others. What is commonly called *religious experience*, before, and during, and after conversion,
comprehends all the elements of philosophical
observation on the subject of conversion. And
however this phrase, *religious experience*, may
be eschewed, and despised as religious *cant*, by
persons addicted to levity, such a treatment of
the human mind is equally derogatory to the
sobriety of the Christian, and to the dignity of
the philosopher. Mental phenomena, in what
ever attitudes, and in relation to whatever subject, are always grave materials of philosophic
observation. How much more to the Christian,
when the mind is coming to and emerging from

the crisis of its conversion to God?—If, indeed, there be anything claiming respect in the whole history of mind, it is its attitudes and sentiments, when looking up to God—when looking into eternity, into heaven, into hell, and endeavouring to settle the question of its destiny in those boundless regions. And he who can sport himself with such a scene, is by no means to be envied for such an exemption from sympathy; but greatly to be pitied for his profane levity, in his treatment of the gravest subject, which ever challenged the attention of man.

Especially is this a field for the most careful and the minutest observation of the minister of religion—of him, whose especial office it is to win souls to Christ, and conduct them to heaven. Of all men he should know and understand, as far as man can know and understand, the thoughts, and reasonings, and feelings of the awakened, the repenting, and the converted sinner. Let it not be said, that this is forbidden ground, an unexplorable field. It is all open. And the minister of religion is bound to enter there, and explore all its regions, and make himself acquainted with all its recesses. He should know all its susceptibilities, and all its actions, in view of Divine truth, in every stage of the history of its religious affections, from its first religious impressions to its cordial embrace of the overtures of the Gospel, and from that hour to the close of its career of faith and hope, and to the opening of its period of heavenly joy. It is *mind*, with which the minister has to deal —he ministers to the spiritual world—and there is his appropriate field of observation. He stands sentinel in those regions, and there should be his home. And is it not fair to suppose, that the minister will be qualified and skilful in his office, just in proportion to the accuracy and extent of his observation here?

And as to the operations of the Spirit, although we cannot comprehend the modes, we may yet observe their effects. And although the office of the Spirit is high and above our reach, the duty of the sinner and the Christian is defined and intelligible. It must be intelligible, in order to be done. Who would presume to advocate a system of duty for man, which can be discharged only by a series of fortuitous accidents—or into which man is to be guided, as if blindfold, by a miraculous influence? Every stage of the sinner's duty is defined and intelligible—(if it can be said that there are stages, as more than one)—as well as that of the Christian. And although God, in the provisions of the Gospel,—that is, in its entire economy—has come so near to man, as to answer all man's necessities, and as to reserve to himself the glory of the sinner's salvation, he has wisely declined to supersede human agency. In other words—God has declined to act in the place of man. He has declined to think, and to feel, and to choose, and to repent, and to believe for him—and all other appropriate parts of man's agency. But all that man *needs* to be done for him, as a sinner, God has supplied, and is ready to bestow—at his instance.

The sinner needs pardon. He must repent. He needs to be born again. He must desire it. He needs the impropriation of the righteousness of Christ to his benefit. He must believe in Christ. But as sinners are disinclined and slow to perform these duties, it is the office of the Christian ministry to *persuade* them—to set before them the light of truth, the duty of repentance, and the great sacrifice for sin. And when this office of the ministry is well and truly done, sinners are ordinarily awakened to serious reflection;—and when awakened, they are likely to pray;—and when they pray, there is hope for their conversion. Sinners, then, must be persuaded to think; (and that is not impossible,) and they must think enough to feel; (and that may be,) and they must feel enough to act;—and they must act in earnest. And all this is within the appropriate sphere of human agency. And it is certain, that God will not be deficient on his part, in all that belongs to the office of the Spirit.

It is a question proper to be made—it is a practical question:—What is the reason, or reasons, why there are so few conversions, where there is so much preaching of the Gospel, and so many means are employed, as in these days? —Why is it that a religion, combining and thoroughly furnished with elementary powers, sufficient for the renovation of the world—sufficient in the proper organization and use of its instrumentalities, to cause a nation to be born in a day—why is it, that such a religion should gain its marches, by such slow degrees, since its ministrations passed from the hands of the Apostles?—Is this question to be resolved in the sovereignty of God, without any default of man?

What I have intended by these suggestions is—a recognition of the adaptation of Christianity, including both the word and Spirit, as a system of means and agencies, to the moral constitution and economy of human nature, as exhibited under its present character and wants; —and that just in proportion as that is understood and applied by the instrumental agents of Christianity, will be the success and triumphs of its ministrations, and that not to detract at all from the glory of God, or to increase the pride and importance of man. It will still be true as ever, and equally within the scope of the doctrines of Revelation—' that the excellency of the power is of God.' The Christian religion could not advance one inch without the Spirit, nor is it intended that the Spirit shall convert one sinner without the means. The means constitute the connexion between the operating cause and the end. And the skilful selection and earnest application of these means, are no unimportant part of the philosophy of religion.

I cannot forbear here, and I hope it will not be considered impertinent, to make a few observations on what are called *sudden* conversions. It is not without reason, that much suspicion and strong prejudices have been entertained against such conversions, on account of many unfortunate and forced results of mere animal excitement, which have been called by this name, and which have justly turned out to their great discredit. It is to be lamented, indeed, that any parts of the Christian world are accustomed to employ such measures, in their persuasive efforts for impenitent sinners, as to be liable to these results, and to occasion this scandal. These facts have led many Christians, and some of the best of ministers, almost, if not quite, to the adoption of the principle—that sudden conversions are never to be trusted. It is to be hoped, that such persons will have the candour to allow of a brief argument on this subject.

It is perhaps well known, that in revivals of religion conversions are often very sudden. And it cannot surely be out of mind, that conversions were ordinarily sudden under the ministry of the Apostles. The three thousand conversions of the day of Pentecost appear all to have taken place during the sittings of one assembly. And all the revivals of religion, if they may be so termed, which occurred during the first age, seem to have been characterized by conversions of this sort. We have reason to suppose it was a common every-day occurrence, under the ministry of the Apostles. It must be allowed, then, that sudden conversions may be genuine—that there is nothing in this fact of itself to invalidate them.

It may be further observed, philosophically and theologically, that conversion, strictly speaking, considered as the turning of the heart, the act or suffering of regeneration, is not only sudden, but instantaneous — that we cannot reckon a passage of time in the sinner's being born again. He was unborn—he is born. But who could find him when he is neither? Conversion, however, considered as an amendment of life, and the formation of a new character, by a set of new habits established by use, is another thing. But this, I take it, is not the thing we are inquiring about. The question is—whether a sinner is born again?—which, to be sure, is to be proved by the conversion of his life. But that is to be expected, if he is really born again. And the new birth cannot occupy time.

Again: there is no reason in philosophy, why conversion, in this sense of it, should not be sudden. Its being sudden, or otherwise, after the mind is first awakened, depends upon the amount of moral forces, impelling it to conversion, which are brought to act upon it. The opposite of a sudden conversion, I suppose, must be the protracted condition of an awakened mind—a protracted serious consideration of the subject of religion, before the mind comes, or is brought to repentance, to a real change of heart, to regeneration. In other words—a protracted suspension of the question in a sinner's mind, whether he will repent, or not?—whether he will obey God, or not?—whether he will submit to Christ, or not?—And those, who object to sudden conversions, would seem to maintain, that the longer the sinner holds this question in suspense, the better. Or how long will they say? —A year?—He may be dead, and in hell, in half that time. Six months?—The same objection lies here. One month?—One week?— One day?—*One hour?*—The same objection lies still. Can he safely, and without disobeying God, to the peril of everlasting damnation, continue *one moment* in a state of impenitence?— The *more* sudden a conversion, then, the better. *Immediate* repentance, on the present instant, is the only safe course—the very and the only requisition of the Gospel.

As I said—the suddenness of conversion, or otherwise, depends upon the amount of moral forces acting upon the mind, and impelling it to repentance. A sinner, for instance, seems to be awakened. He thinks seriously on the subject of religion. He talks with his minister, and gets advice. He goes to his closet, and reads his Bible, and prays. He continues in this course some weeks, perhaps months, it may be a year. And in the meantime nothing is decided. He improves, however. He perseveres, and seems to be coming nearer to the establishment of his character, as a Christian. He is not very powerfully excited at any time. By and by he hopes he is qualified, and is approved and received into the church; and it is to be hoped he is really converted. It may be so. And is this the better way of conversion? Is this obeying God? And where are the rest of a numerous congregation going to, allowing even that there are a half-dozen, or twenty, habitually in such a course of training?—Alas for them!

Now, when we look at conversion merely as moral philosophers, without violating our cha-

racter as Christians, and consider it as comprehending all the stages of serious reflection and
inquiry, of conviction of sin, and anxiety to be
reconciled to God through Jesus Christ, from
the first arrest of the mind, in its thoughtless
and irreligious career, until the heart is supposed
to be renovated by the Spirit of God—(which
doubtless constitutes that view of conversion,
under which objections against *suddenness* arise)
—it will be evident that the mind is hastened, or
is comparatively slow, in coming to that point of
submission to God, at which regeneration may
reasonably be supposed to occur,—according to
the amount and force of motives, which urge it
to that condition. The length and breadth of
the question, then, seems to me to be this:—
whether it is better, that the motives to repentance should be so grouped, accumulated, concentrated, and forced upon the attention and
upon the heart, as to induce *immediate* repentance,—or whether it is better, that the motives
should be so scattered, and so comparatively
inefficient, as to suspend the crisis, and throw it
at a greater distance? This, I think, is the
whole of the exact question. I assume of course
—(for I have no time to make an argument

against those who deny it)—that there is a point, to which all the motives and agencies of Christianity are designed and tend to bring the sinner, making the crisis of his submission to God, and of his regeneration by the Spirit of God, and which in fact constitutes his real and actual conversion.

If those who object to sudden conversions, mean by conversion all those stages of serious reflection which lead to repentance, comprehending also the institution and confirmation of all those habits of life, which go to the formation of Christian character before the world, there can reasonably be no difference of opinion upon the subject. It is evident to every one, that all this must take time. Except, I think, every Christian must allow—the sooner a sinner comes to repentance, the sooner he is born again—the better. And of course, in the sense of immediate, instant repentance, or turning of the heart to God, the more sudden, the better. So that on either of these suppositions, there ought to be no difference.

In revivals of religion, as I have defined and described them, it may easily be conceived, that the moral forces, acting upon the minds of

awakened sinners, and urging them to repentance, are unusually great and powerful. All
the motives and sanctions of religion are accumulated and concentrated. Public sympathy is
roused, and acts with all its accumulating and
subduing powers. And to crown all, and to
account for all, the Spirit of God, which originated this movement, which brought over the
public mind this peculiar atmosphere, which
seems to have charged the whole region with a
supernal and invisible influence, presses truth
upon the conscience with irresistible power, and
penetrates the heart with arrows from the quiver
of the Almighty. Wherever the awakened sinner looks, whether into his own heart or backward on his life, whether into his Bible, or upon
the countenance of his neighbour, or upon an
assembled and weeping congregation, or upon
the man of God who reads to him a violated
law, or into eternity, or up to heaven, or down
to hell—everywhere he sees nothing but motives
to repentance—from every quarter they stare
him in the face, and challenge, by the most
imperative and fearful sanctions, his immediate
return and submission to God. And the Spirit
of God, the while, is moving upon him, pouring

into his mind the light of truth and of eternity, quickening and rousing his conscience, and powerfully exciting his interest for the adjustment of his peace with God, and the settlement of his eternal state.   He weeps in secret places, he groans and agonizes under the action and weight of his guilt, and prays for deliverance. And is it strange, that in such circumstances, and under all these forces, he should come quickly to a decision of the question—whether he will serve God or Mammon?—whether he will devote himself to Christ, or remain devoted to the world?—whether he will surrender to, or hold out against Him, who is the Lord of his being, and who claims to be the sovereign of his affections?—Surely it ought not to be a scandal, that conversions, in such circumstances, are sudden.   If it be looked at merely with the eye and heart of a philosopher, it might easily be seen that it must be so—that it could not be otherwise.   Can man hold out against his God, when God himself lays his own hand upon him, and claims his submission *now*, by all the sanctions of his name and authority, and by the fear of his eternal displeasure?

Conversion, I think, should not be regarded

as a mystery—should not be covered with a cloud, as a thing which cannot be looked into. It is a plain, common-sense, practical business, intelligible to all. It is a decision in mind and heart of the simplest question :—' Shall I love and serve God, or shall I love and serve the world ?'

It has seemed to me proper and not unimportant, to introduce somewhere—and here perhaps is as fit a place as any—a word on one feature of the treatment of awakened sinners, which, so far as I know, is a principle with those ministers in the United States, who have had most experience, and who have been most successful in revivals; and that is—that awakened sinners are not to be consoled, until their pardon is sealed upon the conscience by the Holy Ghost. Such are their views of conversion, that they expect it will manifest itself by such a sense and such tokens of pardoning mercy, and of acceptance with God, rendered to the subject by the Holy Spirit, that ordinarily he can no longer be unhappy, if he would. Instead of depression and weeping, his countenance is lighted up by the radiance of inward peace. For ministers to attempt to console awakened and anxious souls, and to say—*peace* to them, when *God* hath not spoken peace,—while they are yet insubordinate to God, and impenitent, and refuse to trust and leave themselves in the hands of Christ—is considered very dangerous—that it may establish their hopes upon a false foundation, and they notwithstanding live and die without genuine conversion. Ordinarily it is considered, that ministers and Christians have nothing to do in consoling awakened sinners—that their office is instrumentally to convince them of their sin, and guilt, and danger—to present to them all possible motives to induce their repentance—to point them to the Cross, as their only hope—and that God will take care, when once they have made submission to him, through Jesus Christ, that they are suitably consoled. And such proves to be the fact. The Holy Ghost is ordinarily a satisfactory Comforter, when once the heart has submitted. He is the best Comforter—the only Comforter that should be relied upon *.

It may sometimes happen, indeed, where persons have been habitually the subjects of

* See Chapter XIII.

morbid affections of the mind, induced by physical causes,—or where the habitual temperament is exceedingly diffident and distrustful of
its own feelings—or where, combined with such
causes, or without them, some wrong notions of
conversion and of experimental religion, have
been deeply imbibed—in such cases, it may
happen, that persons apparently and really en-
titled to hope in the settlement of their peace
with God, do notwithstanding refuse to hope,
and continue to mourn and repine. Judgment
and discretion are requisite in the treatment of
such cases. It may not only be necessary to
console them, but to use all possible endeavours to demolish all their reasonings against
themselves, and to establish their hope in Christ.
If they are evidently afflicted by a physical
malady, tending to such depressions of mind, it
may be necessary to divert them by physical
means, and by healthful moral exercises. But
nine cases out of ten, and perhaps in a greater
proportion, anxious minds are not to be hastily
consoled by man. But they should be urged
to repentance, they should be forced from every
refuge of lies, until encompassed by and feelin
the necessities of their case, they shall be morally

compelled to throw themselves, in a last, forlorn hope, into the only sure refuge. And when they have got there, they will not need consolation from man—the Holy Ghost shall be their Comforter.

Adjunct to this is the principle—that the awakening and conversion of sinners should be the grand labour of ministers and of the Church. And this is doubtless the most efficient method of promoting the edification of the Church, and its confirmation in the orthodoxy of the Bible. Speculative truth lodged in the mind will be comparatively of little effect, so long as its impressions are not engraved upon the heart, and incorporated with its affections, by exercise towards its proper objects. What is more common, than nominal Christians, of the unsoundest heart, holding an orthodox creed, so long as they are not disturbed by it? And when they are disturbed, there will be no little danger, that they will make shipwreck of their faith. The only sure way to secure the foundations of orthodoxy, is by the promotion, and circulation, and active energy of vital religion. It would be a libel on Christianity to suppose, that religion of the heart is

in danger of injuring the religion of the head,
—that they who read the Bible most, and pray
most, and agonize most for the conversion of
sinners, are more likely, on that account, to
imbibe errors of Christian doctrine. And it is
a consummate paradox, that the prosperity of
religion, in the enlargement of the Church,
will be its blighting. It is right feeling that
most effectually secures right thinking. A
heart turned to God, and that looks to God, is
most likely to be associated with a mind enlightened and taught of God.

I will take the liberty of introducing here a
brief narrative, appertaining to the subject of
sudden conversions, the facts of which were
parts of my own experience and observation,
and the scene entirely remote from any general
and public excitement. Some half dozen years
ago, I was called to preach on a Sabbath morning to one of the largest congregations in a
principal city of the United States—a congregation, in which, so far as I know, there had never
been a religious excitement of the nature of a
revival, and in which at the time there was no
special feeling. As I descended from the pulpit
to retire, in company with the retiring congre-

gation, I accidentally perceived, in a remote part of the church, a well-dressed and good-looking man, with his eye fixed on me, and making his way towards me, against the current of the crowd. The first glance at his countenance showed, that his feelings had been and still continued in great agitation. He did not turn away his eye, but pressed forward, and was soon directly before me. He instantly grasped my hand, his whole frame convulsed by inward emotion, and said with difficulty, and in a faultering voice :—' Sir, will you pray for me?' And then, bursting into tears, was forced to lay his head upon a pew to support himself. It was a novel and an affecting scene, and attracted considerable attention, as many of the congregation were still around us. Perceiving his extreme agitation, I felt that he had need to be seated, and proposed to him, that we should enter and sit down in the pew. ' Any where—any where,' said he. Misunderstanding me, he conceived I had proposed to comply with his request in that place, and immediately was moving into the pew. Not deeming it exactly proper to engage in prayer, in such circumstances of a retiring crowd, I changed the pro-

posal, and offered to accompany him home—
and took his arm, and went to his house. On
the way he made many apologies,—expressed
himself sorry his feelings were so overcome,—
said he could not help it,—and along with the
exhibition of other feelings, seemed to be mor-
tified. But all the way he trembled with agitation. His wife had remained at home that
morning. And when we entered the house, not
knowing my name, and being so overcome, he
was unable to introduce me,—and immediately
sat down, laying his face in his hands, and
leaning on a table, wept aloud in the presence
of his wife. Aware of the natural effect of such
surprise, as his wife rose from her chair with
evident emotion and concern, I lost no time in
signifying to her the occasion. She stopped,
lifted up her hands and eyes to heaven, and then
clasping her hands, burst into tears of gratitude—and said : ‘This is what I have been
praying for.’ At this instant her husband rose
from his seat, came to my side, and taking hold
of my arm, was struggling to speak, but unable. His wife embraced him, and begged him
to be composed. At this moment we all stood
by the side of a sofa, alike involved in the

scene, but each probably moved by very different feelings. Struggling still with his emotions, he finally gave utterance to this single monosyllable, evidently wishing to say more, but there stopped : 'Pray——,' said he. And immediately, without waiting, kneeled down, by the side of the sofa, and laid his face upon it in his hands. And what could *we* do, at such a sight ? —*We* kneeled down involuntarily, his wife on one side of him, endeavouring to support his agitated frame—and myself on the other, trying to pray. Any one may imagine the difficulty of arming the tongue for utterance in such circumstances. My words were few, and broken, and far between. And when I rose from my knees, he did not rise, and his wife could not rise. Who can fully appreciate such a scene, without having been a witness ? I looked upon them, as I rose —and thought it was a scene, which might well move the heart of God. And so it did. Soon, however, we were all seated, and having engagements for the afternoon, I left this man what I deemed suitable advice, and retired, promising to call in the evening.

I called,—and found the man composed, his countenance bright and free from every tear, his heart apparently content and happy. He received me with great cordiality, and was ready to enter immediately upon conversation, unembarrassed and with perfect freedom;—the subject, however, was another from what he had been accustomed. He could think of nothing, speak of nothing, but the scenes of the day, and the hand of God, which, in so brief a time, had made this world to him all a new world. He asked me, among other things, if I could recommend to him some suitable religious books. I mentioned 'Doddridge's Rise and Progress.' 'Here it is,' said he; 'Mr. ——, one of the elders of the Church,' (who had witnessed the scene of the morning in the church) 'brought it in his pocket this afternoon, and gave it to me after service.' 'A remarkable coincidence,' said I.

I spent the evening with this man with great satisfaction, heard the history of his life, and have never seen him since. About a year afterwards I wrote to a friend in the same city, to inquire after him, and received the answer from himself—in which he gave me the history of his life since the eventful day—an account of his baptism—of his joining himself with the people of God, and of the holy satisfactions of a religious life. And if I am ever so happy as to attain heaven, I shall expect to meet him there —and that he will probably date his conversion on the day of the scenes just described.

It may be interesting, and important to the merits of this case, to know something of the former character and history of this man. He had lived, ' of the straitest sect, a pharisee'— was blessed with an exemplary and amiable wife, and a family of lovely children—himself a man of good parts — respectable in society — exactly honest in all his dealings—his warmest and best affections centering and bound up in his family. He actually made a religion of his love and care for his family, of his honesty towards men, and of the regularity of his life. And he came to church, on the morning of the day, which has furnished the materials of this narrative, a perfect Pharisee—though indeed under the pressure of some recent afflictions. And to God be all the glory of the change ! This was a *sudden* conversion, and as perfectly insulated, as is ordinarily possible. I have known hundreds of conversions, as sudden as this, and apparently not the less genuine.

As being in point to the general subject of this chapter, more especially to the latter part of it, and as an historical illustration of the whole, I will conclude by introducing the narrative of an American revival, published in the New York Observer in December last, and communicated, as the editor of that paper observes, ' by a gentleman, holding an important station in that part of the country '—that is, in Jefferson-County, of the State of New York :—

' Jefferson-County, New York, Nov. 1, 1831.

' Sir,

' In addressing you, and, through the medium of your excellent journal, the Christian community at large, it is my object to give a plain and simple history, so far as my knowledge of facts shall enable me, of the displays of Divine power and goodness with which of late our county has been so highly favoured.   Detached and imperfect accounts of this work of the Lord in particular churches have already gone abroad; but viewing as I do the unusual attention to eternal things which has been manifested in several of our churches, as produced by one general outpouring of God's Spirit, I deem it proper that this account should be a general one of the revival in *Jefferson-County.* And that hereby the riches of God's grace may be magnified—his name honoured—the hearts of the Lord's people encouraged, is my most humble and most earnest prayer.

' For some time previous to any remarkable excitement, there was evident in some of our churches an increased attention to holy things; a deeper spirit of piety seemed to pervade the bosoms of Christ's professed followers, and a marked reverence for the ordinances of the sanctuary was observed. Many had presentiments of great things about to be performed. The devout Christian especially exercised strong faith in *Him,* who is not slack concerning his promises.

'At a period so propitious, when circumstances seemed to warrant and even demand extraordinary effort, a *protracted* * meeting was commenced in the village of Adams. Deep interest for the result was felt by all who sincerely loved the Redeemer's cause, and desired its advancement. Many were the prayers, which were put

* A meeting of a number of days, to which this term, by way of distinction, is ordinarily applied.

up, we trust in faith, in different parts of the county, to the great Head of the Church, that he would crown the meeting with the presence of his Spirit. This was in the month of March last. Public exercises commenced on Tuesday, and were closed on the Sabbath following. During the first three days, the course was such as is commonly adopted in meetings of a similar nature; but on the morning of Friday, so deep and powerful were the feelings of the assembly, that it was deemed expedient to deviate somewhat from the usual method. God had indeed met with his people, and so sensibly was his presence realized, so awfully momentous appeared the responsibilities of the hour, that it was with the greatest difficulty they could refrain from giving vent aloud to the emotions, that swayed their bosoms. Every head was bowed, and every pious heart flowed out to God in deep and fervent supplication. The ear of the Almighty was not deaf to their prayer. The waters of life flowed freely. Anxious meetings * were continued for several days after the public meetings were suspended. It is im-

---

* Meetings for enquiring, anxious sinners, in which they are counselled and prayed for.

possible to state precisely the number of those, who were hopefully converted. Many who came in from a distance, went away rejoicing in the hope of a glorious immortality. Probably more than a hundred were here the subjects of renewing grace.

'Immediately after the meeting at Adams another commenced at Rodman, five miles distant, which continued thirteen days without intermission. Public exercises were held three times a-day, and the usual course was pursued. At this place it is supposed, that nearly two hundred gave evidence of a saving change. During the first three days but little was effected, and the aspect of things was dull and cheerless—but on Thursday the prospect was brightened. The cloud of mercy burst suddenly upon the people, and in the short space of twenty-four hours, rising of thirty expressed a hope of having passed from death unto life. From this time the revival advanced steadily forward until the close of the meeting. The population of this village is small, but so general was the revival, that of the few, scarcely an adult was left unconverted.

'On the day following the close of this meeting

(the 25th of April), a meeting of the converts was held in the village of Adams, which was addressed by the Rev. J. Burchard. Of more than four hundred, who had obtained hope since the revival had commenced in this latter place, three hundred were present. This was a scene of exceeding interest. And when all arose and sung a favourite hymn, we seemed in imagination to catch the faint echoings of the song in the upper sanctuary. This I trust, was a day of happiness to many, which will never be forgotten. It was a blessed antepast of that bliss, which is reserved for the redeemed above.

'On the 2nd of May, a meeting commenced at *Evan's Mills*, about ten miles distant from Watertown, of which Mr. Burchard, who had conducted the two already mentioned, was requested to take the direction. Public exercises were continued uninterruptedly for nine days, during which time, through the blessing of God, about a hundred and twenty-five persons were hopefully converted. On the 17th of the same month, a meeting commenced at Brownville, which continued ten days, and resulted in the hopeful conversion of more than a hundred and fifty souls.

'Immediately upon leaving Brownville, Mr. Burchard returned to his own people at Bellville, to conduct a Union meeting of the Baptist and Presbyterian brethren of that place. In this meeting sectional and party feeling was wholly laid aside, and those of different names met and laboured upon the common footing of Christians and servants of the Most High. They asked for a *large* portion of the Spirit, and measured their desires rather by the power and goodness of God, than by their own weakness and ill desert. Their supplications were heard and answered. The moving of the Spirit was like the sweep of an overwhelming flood, bearing away with resistless energy every obstacle that opposed its progress. The mouth of the gainsayer was stopped, and the enemies of the Cross, confounded and abashed, looked on in mute astonishment. The powers of darkness seemed to have loosened their hold of their victims, and haughty and rebellious men bowed in submission before the offended Majesty of heaven. For two or three days, rising of an hundred each day expressed hope of having been born again. To give an idea of the power of the work, it is sufficient to state that at one time, during a season of prayer in the anxious room, which lasted about fifteen minutes, thirty-seven persons indulged a hope of having passed from death unto life ; all of whom, so far as I have been able to learn, still exhibit in their lives evidence of the reality of the change.

' The village of Bellville itself is small, there being not more than fifty houses ; but the people in great numbers came in from the surrounding country. It is impossible to ascertain the exact number of those who obtained hope during the meeting *. Individuals who were engaged in the work, and who were enabled from actual observation to form tolerably correct estimates, suppose the number to be not less than six or seven hundred. The lowest estimate I have heard, would place it between five and six hundred. The meeting, which continued twelve days, closed on the Sabbath, and on the Tuesday following, another commenced at Champion, which lasted seven days, during which time one hundred and fifty persons obtained hope of eternal life.

' From this place Mr. Burchard went to

* *Protracted* meeting.

Woodville, a small settlement three miles from Bellville, of about thirty families. This meeting commenced on Friday, and continued till Tuesday of the next week. The anxious room was open until Thursday, when about seventy gave evidence of a saving change. The subjects of this work were, with few exceptions, persons of adult age; many in the middle age of life, and several who had numbered their threescore and ten.

' The general characteristics of this work have been deep conviction of sin, followed by an early surrender * of the heart to God. Among its subjects are persons of every class and every age. Men of the highest standing have not been ashamed to profess themselves disciples of the Cross, and of the many who, since the commencement of these meetings, have obtained hope in Christ, there are but very few who do not stand fast in the faith, and give satisfactory evidence of a change of heart.

' The means made use of have been the prayer of faith, the preaching of the word in a plain and practical manner, pressing home upon the

* That is—*sudden* conversion.

sinner's conscience his guilt before God, and the duty of *immediate* repentance *.'

———————

This letter is a practical comment on the grand subject of this volume, itself, perhaps, claiming some comments from me. The scene of this revival is an agricultural region, and a remote county in the state of New York, with a sparse population, comprehending only a trifling fraction of the numerous and widely-extended communities, in that and other States of the Union, which have experienced like refreshing visitations of the Spirit of God, within a year and some months past. This little narrative I hope will be understood, in connexion with the discussions and presentations of the previous chapters. It may be recollected that I have in several instances alluded generally to the manner of conducting American revivals, and to the *pro-tracted* public meetings, extending through a number of days, which are held for the purpose of promoting revivals, or as the exigencies of public feeling may demand. It will have been

* See Chapter XIII. for an extended notice of this kind of preaching.

observed, that meetings are spoken of in this letter, as having been protracted, *five, six, seven, nine, ten, twelve,* and in one instance, *thirteen* days, ' without intermission.' It is not to be understood, that such meetings are continued more than a week by any previous appointment—rarely so much as a week. But it is the exigencies of this state of public feeling, for the time being, which occasion them; and they are protracted at the discretion of the ministers and influential Christians, who superintend and conduct them. When the Spirit of God descends upon a community, as on some of these occasions, the public interest increasing every day, the number of the anxious and inquiring multiplying in every direction, and souls hopefully born again from day to day, and from hour to hour;—when every meeting and every labour are evidently and greatly blessed, it is impossible, in consistence with duty, it would be criminal, to repulse the weeping applications, coming in from all quarters : ' Sirs, what must I do to be saved ? '—' Men and brethren, what shall we do ? '—It is the harvest-time of souls. And there can be no question, that these anxious and perishing souls should be attended to, till their peace is made with God, before any thing else. There needs no apology for suspending all other business, in such an hour, for such an object, until the words of the Saviour—' Seek first the kingdom of God and his righteousness'—and all the claims of the Gospel, and all the woes of impenitence, are blotted from the inspired records, by the same hand, which placed them there. People at a distance, who have never witnessed such a scene, who have been bred in the chills of a formal religion, who have never seen the agony of an awakened sinner, nor felt the appeals to their hearts of multitudes involved at the same instant in the same condition of mind—who have never sympathised with souls just born again, nor seen their countenance lighted up with the fresh beams of Christian hope, nor heard their voice attuned to the praise of redeeming grace—such people may talk of extravagance, enthusiasm, fanaticism! Alas! they know nothing whereof they affirm. *They* are the men, who are carried away with imagination. All their conceptions of such a scene are the mere creations of fancy. An impenitent sinner's solicitude for reconciliation to God through Jesus Christ, and his earnest prosecution of that object, to the suspension of every other interest, till this is secured, if not the most sober, is certainly the most rational employment, to which he can consecrate his energies. Any thing else, till this is done, is folly and madness. This only is wisdom.

But, under a proper and wise superintendence, there is nothing in these public religious excitements, which anybody has need to fear—nothing, for which the most sober and calculating spirit need entertain a moment's concern; unless, indeed, he is prepared to wish, that a sinner should never be concerned for his own salvation—and with such I have no argument. In a time of general security—imagined security in sin, I mean—it cannot be doubtful among Christians, that all possible and hopeful means should be employed for awakening the careless. In a time of revival, the unawakened should still be regarded for the same purpose, and the awakened should receive all needful attentions. What Christian would not pronounce it wise, the noblest and the highest object, under a hopeful prospect, to suspend all ordinary business of a community, for the salvation of that community?—to suspend all ordinary business of the world, a little season, for the salvation of the world?—And when the Spirit of God has come down, and roused the public mind to the care of eternal things, shall the minister of religion desert his post?—Shall the Church dissolve its sessions of prayer and labour? —and all the professed friends of the Redeemer turn away from the work, which God has thrown upon their hands?—Is not such a state of things worth praying and labouring for?—And when it has come, shall it not be improved?—In the United States, it *is* prayed for, and laboured for. And when it comes in answer to the prayers, and in reward of the labours of Christians, they do not think it needs an apology to improve it. And that it takes so much time, and demands so much labour, cannot be considered a reasonable subject of regret, when weighed against the object;—but rather is it to be regretted, that there is so little of such demand for either.

During the revival at Belleville, as noticed in the letter introduced above, a village of only fifty or sixty families, but visited at the time by people from the surrounding country, it is stated, that ' for two or three days more than *a hundred each day* expressed hope of having been born again. And to give an idea of the power of the work, it is sufficient to state, that at one time, during a season of prayer in the anxious room, which lasted about fifteen minutes, *thirty-seven* persons indulged a hope of having passed from death unto life;—all of whom, so far as I have been able to learn, still exhibit in their lives evidence of the reality of the change.' This letter was dated nearly five months after the scene above described, as may be seen. All the events noticed in this communication occurred five, six, and seven months, previous to its date. The narrative, it will be observed, is sober, and certainly I would not have introduced it here, if I could not honestly commend it as credible, from what I know of such things, both as to the events themselves, and as to the weight due to such communications. No respectable person, such as the writer is declared to be, by the editor, and as the face of his narrative might evince, would risk his reputation in such a statement, if it could not be fully sustained by the facts; as the very paper, in which it is published, circulates in the region where the events occurred.

But I was about to make some comments on the two or three more remarkable things of this narrative, which I had just quoted.—' For two or three days,' at Belleville, ' more than a hundred each day expressed hope of having been born again.' Need I say—that the *expression of a hope,* as here indicated, is the declaration, or acknowledgment of a sensible change of mind, or feeling, supposed to be wrought upon the subject by the Holy Spirit, in consequence, or at the instant, of true repentance—in consequence of the submission of the heart to God—affording a satisfactory and comforting evidence of the Divine favour—that God is reconciled—that the individual's sins are forgiven, and that he is accepted in Christ. In seasons of revival such sensible manifestations are common and expected *,—in some instances very striking and very remarkable, in others not so much so. The change of mind, I mean, is remarkable in the personal experience of the subject. His feelings are changed from anxiety to serenity, from the grief of repentance to the joy of hope. And here I beg leave to refer to observations

* And should they not *always* be expected ?

already made in this chapter on sudden conversions, on the treatment of the anxious, and the comforts of the Spirit, as explanatory of this point. The amount of moral forces concentrated and acting upon the minds of awakened sinners, in seasons of revival, ordinarily brings them to speedy repentance. The work is brief, in proportion as it is powerful.

It is stated in this narrative, that on one occasion, during a season of prayer of fifteen minutes, *thirty-seven* persons were made the subjects of this change of mind from grief to joy, from despondency to hope. What a season! what an amazing influence! and yet, instead of being surprised that it was so great, we should only regret that it was not greater. For doubtless sinners were there, who did not repent, and probably never will. I am not willing here to meet a caviller, who wishes to ask—how could these cases be ascertained? Not, however, because there is any other difficulty, than that of satisfying an unreasonable man. True conversion, as I have in another place remarked, is apt to demonstrate itself, especially in a revival. The soul, that was anxious, is comforted, because he cannot help it.—God has spoken peace

to him, and satisfied his conscience. In a revival ordinarily, a person that has passed this
change of mind, has only need to look up, and
show his face, and everybody sees it. Especially, if he has been deeply anxious, which is
supposed. Every feature of anxiety is erased
from his countenance, and it beams with light
and satisfaction. He, whose head drooped,
whose voice moaned the irrepressible anguish
of his spirit, and whose eyes were red with
weeping, now looks up with a smile. And besides these visible expressions, the free communication of feeling on these occasions always
and speedily ascertains questions of this 'sort.—
He who is born again will tell some Christian
friend ' what God has done for his soul;' and
when and where.

As the narrative, on which these few remarks
have been made, brings to view, in some of its
shapes, the general economy of the most energetic revival-operations in the United States, it
may be proper to spend some additional observations on the subject of *protracted* meetings, as
they are properly termed, which have been extensively introduced for a few years past, and
with great success. It is a special effort for the

revival of religion—it being an appointment agreed upon, for a convention of Ministers and Christians from an extended district, to support a combined and concentrated action of religious influence, in the midst of a particular community for a number of days—ordinarily within the limits of a week. There will be, perhaps, three regular services, with a sermon, each day —the intervals of time being filled up by smaller and more detached meetings, less formal, and for the purposes of prayer and exhortation;—also in visiting from house to house, and making direct personal conversations, and appeals with all, who may be disposed to listen. In these scattered and less formal efforts, the gifts and talents of the more distinguished and useful laymen are brought into action, in conjunction with the labours of ministers, and often with great and good effect. And those, who come in from abroad on these occasions, generally come in the spirit of revival—they come for the special object of a revival, in this particular community— they come with faith, believing that God is disposed and accustomed to own such efforts for this purpose. They know, that he has done it. They themselves have been personal witnesses

of the same operations inducing such results.
There is faith in the church, planted in this community, who have negotiated this arrangement
for this specific object. And there is a general
expectation among the people, that as the same
means have been followed with such consequences
in other places, they are likely to produce the
same effects here. And ministers and Christians all unite in their efforts and in their prayers,
in public and in private, in larger and in smaller
assemblies, addressing themselves, as opportunity
presents, to the hearts and consciences of individuals—all with one single aim—waiting upon
God for his blessing. Religion is thè business
of the time with all, where attention can be
gained. And these assemblies are not ordinarily
dissolved, these efforts are not apt to conclude,
without a great and lasting impression upon the
community. And they are often the means of
an immediate and powerful revival. Sometimes,
as may be observed in this narrative, two, or
three, or more days will have passed away, and
no distinct public impression seems to be made.
The work, in the mean time, labours heavily.
And then, perhaps, a Pentecostal visitation
comes. The Spirit of God descends *evidently,*

and with greater power, upon the people. All feel it. The fervour and importunity of prayer increase. And sinners begin to be awakened in every direction. Instances of hopeful conversion daily, and perhaps hourly, occur. And now a work, a great work, has fallen upon the ministers and people of God. And the state of the public mind may imperatively demand, that they should continue in this field for many days. To desert it would evidently be deserting the post of duty, to which the providence of God has obviously called them. The soil is now made mellow, and the seed should be sown; there is now a hearing ear, and the word must be preached; the heart is open, and the opportunity should be embraced; the condition of multitudes of anxious and inquiring souls, demands that they should be instructed and guided; new converts must be ascertained and confirmed; those who are yet careless need to be admonished; and there may be sufficient and urgent reasons for extending this great religious solemnity an indefinite time. It is a harvest of souls—it is a revival of religion.

CHAPTER XIII.

THE MODE OF PREACHING IN THE UNITED STATES, WHICH HAS SEEMED TO BE MOST HONOURED, AS A MEANS OF THE CONVERSION OF SINNERS, AND OF PROMOTING REVIVALS.

On pages 75 and 219, 220 of this volume I have had occasion, incidentally, in the former case, to prescribe a treatment of awakened sinners ; and in the latter to declare it, as characteristic of those ministers in the United States, who have been most experienced and most successful in revivals of religion. Since those pages have gone to press, and are placed beyond my power of enlargement, or exposition, in those places, I have had some occasion to apprehend, that more might possibly be inferred from those brief and naked statements, than I had intended; and this apprehension has in truth given birth to the present chapter, and must make my apology for its introduction here. And although it was not a part of my original plan, yet perhaps after all it will not be unacceptable, or out of place. As the whole work is intended to answer inquiries of British Christians, and give them information on the general subject, I am reminded in this place, that the question has often been made to me,—whether there is any peculiar mode of preaching in the United States, which may be supposed instrumental in promoting revivals?—And as there is some difficulty and some delicacy in attempting to answer this question, I did not purpose to make the answer a component element of this volume, until I came to this place, and had taken advice, in view of the reason already specified, and of some other considerations, which have come before me.

I beg leave also farther to premise, that neither in the remarks of this chapter, nor of any other, do I profess to be the organ of the American religious public; but am willing to be regarded, as writing on my own personal responsibility, which is the simple truth. It is possible, and not unlikely, that others, entertaining similar views with myself, in a like attempt, would have expressed themselves somewhat differently. All I profess is—honesty of purpose—a wish to gratify inquiry—and an humble attempt, if God shall please so to order, to do some little good, in contributing, if possible, to the revival of Evangelical religion, by a declaration, on this side of the Atlantic, of some of the great and good things, which God has done for the American Churches. And as God is pleased to honour a faithful ministry for the revival of religion, I am aware, that the subject of this chapter must be intrinsically interesting, and perhaps not the least important of the several topics, which have come under consideration. And I profess on the threshold—that it is most distant from any consent of my heart to assume the office of instruction, or of rebuke—or to do anything more, than to meet inquiries; and in this way, if possible, to be in some measure useful. At the same time, I hope and trust, I shall be allowed the privilege of supporting any opinion, which it may seem necessary for me to avow in the execution of such a design, without being supposed willing to make controversy with dissentients, if any there should be, among those who may be inclined to look into these pages.

One other preliminary remark: it is undoubtedly true, that there is every kind of preaching, and every grade of excellence in this office, in the United States, as in all other Christian countries. And I could not conscientiously say, so far as my observation has extended, that any particular kind, or mode of preaching, in that country, has *exclusively* prevailed, where revivals of religion have occurred. On the contrary, revivals have prevailed in multitudes of places, where, comparatively, the character of the preaching, though generally orthodox and faithful, has yet been very diverse: —in one place, where the preaching has been almost exclusively doctrinal; in another, where it has been rather exhortatory, than didactic; in some instances, where a particular set of doctrines have been made prominent—in others, another set of doctrines—the preaching, however, as a whole, in either case, involving the essential elements of the Gospel. And in some instances revivals have occurred, where the preaching was anything but Evangelical—downright heresy, by the common consent of the orthodox Christian world. In the latter case, however, it has been apparently by the providential introduction of the Gospel, in spite of the efforts of heresy to keep it out. And the effect has been to renovate such communities, and to establish Evangelical preaching among them.

It must doubtless be allowed, that revivals have occurred in the United States, under all these and other varying prominent character-istics of preaching. At the same time, it is also to be remarked, that a revival not only controls the character of preaching for the time being, whatever it may have been before, so as to produce a very great uniformity—but it con-trols it afterwards, in the same tendency to uni-formity. It produces an appetite in the popular mind for the most awakening considerations, which the whole system of Christian doctrine combines. And nothing else, and nothing less will satisfy the public mind, in such a state of feeling. And wherever there is a faithful mi-nistry, it not only falls in with this demand, but takes lead in such a career, imbibes a warmer spirit, receives a new impulse, operates with in-creased energy, and in the degree of manifold success. A revival often gives a minister, who was orthodox and allowed to be faithful before, an entire new character, so that the lustre and success of his subsequent career throw all his former efforts into the shade. Nobody impeaches what he was, while everybody sees, that he is another and a better man—a more faithful, more energetic, and more successful minister of Christ. He has caught a holier fire from the inner sanctuary—the sanctuary of a revival. Generally, the season of a revival, and the effect of it upon the popular mind, demand and inspire a uniform character of preaching—preaching of a higher tone—more awakening to the sinner, more edifying to the Christian, more energetic upon the conscience universally, whether the conscience be good or bad. Revivals have renovated communities, renovated churches, and renovated ministers. They have made good ministers out of bad ones, and good ones better,— they have in multitudes of instances, and extensively, changed the character of preaching, and elevated it radically, essentially, greatly. They have given to it unwonted power, and unexampled success. And there is doubtless a reciprocal influence of revivals on preaching, and of preaching on revivals. And it is with the latter, that I have promised more especially to have to do in the present chapter. And I hope it will not be thought, that these preliminary observations are impertinent, which, I confess, have well nigh threatened to occupy the principal place.

I trust I have sufficiently allowed, that no particular mode of preaching has been *exclusively* instrumental in promoting revivals of religion—or more properly, in originating them—so far as the facts and places of their occurrence would go to demonstrate*. But after all this allowance is made, I think myself justified in saying, that the most prominent and most successful revival ministers in the United States are characterized by a somewhat uniform mode of preaching, which is not beyond the reach of definition; that this kind of preaching is instrumentally created by revivals, and itself in turn instrumentally reproduces its own instrumental cause; and that the amount of it, in this way, is gradually increasing, and itself multiplying the amount of its own influence. I

---

* It would be a mistake to conclude that any visible means, immediately preceding a revival, and contemporaneous with it, are of course, and in all instances, the *effectual* means—although they may seem to have been so. For although it is an undoubted truth, that God honours fidelity, it is equally true, that he does not make that the sole condition, nor the limit or measure of the outpourings of his Spirit.

state it of course simply as the honest conviction of my own observation. And it is my individual opinion, that this is the prominent and leading influence, in sustaining and promoting revivals in the United States, so far as instrumentality is concerned. I have some hesitation, indeed, whether I can reduce this influence to the form of a definition in a single sentence, so as fully to comprehend and indicate it. But if I should fail in this, I shall hope that subsequent observations may supply the deficiency.

I would say, then, that this mode of preaching is characterized by a studious effort to combine the cardinal principles both of original and evangelical law, and a persevering application of those principles, in their various Scriptural forms, through the understanding and reason, to the consciences of sinners, until they come to repentance.

I trust I need not say, that what I mean by *original and evangelical law*, is what is commonly called *the law and the Gospel*. My reason for throwing it into this form is, to express simply the obligations of both upon the conscience, as *law*—it being assumed (for I have not time to make an argument), that the preaching especially applicable to impenitent sinners, is the obligation of these two several codes. And this mode of preaching will of course involve both the law and the Gospel, in all their scope and variety. And the peculiarity * of it consists in this: that the whole is brought before the mind of the sinner for the especial purpose of convincing him of his *obligation* to both these codes—it being also assumed, that the Gospel is not only a provision, a remedy, but that it comes clothed with all the sanctions of law, as truly and as much as the institutes of the Decalogue; that the command to repent and to believe is as imperative and as penal, as the command to love God, or any branch of the moral law. ' God now *commandeth* all men everywhere to repent.' The very showing of the full and

---

* Not that the preaching I am now describing is *altogether* peculiar to American ministers. Although it is, perhaps, probable, that it makes more especially a reigning characteristic of those ministers in the United States, who are more earnestly engaged in promoting revivals of religion. But so far as this may be allowed to be faithful preaching, I should esteem it ungenerous, and contrary to truth, to claim it, as exclusively employed by Christian ministers of my own country. I wish it to be understood, that I am only asserting facts in one place, without denying their existence in another, or even implying their absence.

abounding mercy of the Gospel, (which of course is not to be withheld) and in all its exceeding and infinite richness, is only another and an indirect demonstration of the impenitent sinner's exceeding and infinite guilt in rejecting it. And the greater the mercy, the richer the grace, the more generous the offer—the greater his guilt. To the impenitent sinner, therefore, the conscience-appealing language of the Gospel is,—' If the word ministered by angels was steadfast, and every transgression and disobedience received a just recompense of reward—how shall *ye* escape, if ye neglect so *great salvation?*' ' If he who despised *Moses'* law, perished without mercy under two or three witnesses, of how much *sorer* punishment shall *he* be thought worthy, who has trampled under feet the Son of God! and counted the blood of the covenant wherewith he was sanctified an unholy thing! and done despite unto the Spirit of Grace!' ' Of how much *sorer* punishment !' The law is hard enough, but the Gospel is harder, to the disobedient. Under the law there is no protection,—under the Gospel there is still less protection to an impenitent sinner, to an unbeliever. ' He that believeth not, is condemned *already*. The wrath of God *abideth* on him.' Every principle of the Gospel writes against him a deeper damnation—dooms him to a lower chamber of the pit of eternal woe. Every bowel of tenderness, which the Gospel opens to him, only proves him more worthy of hell. Bring out the Gospel, then, in all its entireness—withhold not a single iota. Propound its overture—spread out all its promises—declare all its richness; to the impenitent sinner, to the unbeliever, it is a law of doom—a stronger, a more fearful law, than any that ever was read to him. It makes him an offer, indeed; but by the very supposition of his character, he declines it. Set up the Cross, and show him a bleeding, dying Saviour, and tell him—tell him with beseeching importunity—tell him with tears—here ' is blood that cleanseth from all sin.' But, by the very supposition of his character, he has refused it—and still refuses. It may be, however, that he will be moved—that he will weep—that he will give up his heart. Try him—try him continually— try him to the last moment of his probation; but do not deceive him. And so long as he refuses, is there a law or a Gospel in the universe, which God has promulgated, from which can

lawfully be read a word of consolation to him?
—There is *encouragement* on a condition—but
the condition is refused and trampled on.

I am unwilling it should be understood, from
the remarks I have made in former chapters,
of the treatment suitable to sinners, and to awakened sinners—and from having attributed such
treatment, as a prominent characteristic of the
preaching of ministers in the United States,
who have been most successful in promoting
revivals—or from the drift of the argument, in
which I am now engaged—that such preaching
especially involves the *terrific*, in distinction
from the *tender*. Far from it. I cannot honestly be an advocate of that style of declamatory preaching, which tends rather to astound,
than to convince—rather to shock the nervous
system, than to probe the conscience. The former is not the style of preaching to which I refer.
And nothing would be more unjust than for me
to declare it, as the prevailing character of that
class of ministers, of whom I am now speaking.
There is not, perhaps, a set of ministers in the
world, of more temperate and sober feeling, more
exact in the study of their language for the
pulpit, and for the discharge of all their public

and private official functions, than those of New England, and some other parts of our country, who for a century past, and especially of late years, have been called in the providence of God to minister in revivals of religion, and who have maintained a leading influence in the religious excitements of the age. Nor have these excitements, in any degree, thrown them from the steady balance of their characteristic sobriety. It is not declamation—it is not the noise they have made, that has given them their influence. It is not the preaching of *terror*, in the common acceptation of this term. For terror cannot, of itself, be an instrument, nor an element of Evangelical conviction. But it is pouring the light of truth into the understanding—it is informing the judgment—it is appealing to the bar of reason—it is producing a sober conviction of mind —and through the medium of those faculties, whose province it is to weigh thoughts, and to make rational deductions, to leave the message of the eternal God with the conscience—to *leave* it there. And there it works—there it produces uneasiness, and allows of no quiet, until the great question—until the controversy between God and the sinner, is settled. And this uneasiness is demonstrated, even in a revival, not by clamour, not by confusion, not by running to and fro, as if men did not know what they were doing. But it is shown by serious and solemn reflection, by the introversion of the mind. Sometimes, indeed, there is great agitation of conscience. But the subject of it can give a reason—he sees, he apprehends the reasons. He has come to this state of mind by the most rational deductions. And if he ever reasoned correctly, he reasons correctly now—and in this sense soberly, notwithstanding he may be the subject of the most pungent distress.

And what does the minister do, at such a time —the minister that appreciates the responsibility of his treatment of such minds—the minister, that is ' *wise* in winning souls to Christ?' Does he presume to *detract* from the motives, which are now urging the sinner to repentance?— awful, awful would be his responsibility, to do so. The very fact, that the sinner is still impenitent, and only anxious, proves that the force of these motives is yet inadequate to the desired result.

It is supposed, that the preaching, which has brought the sinner to this state of mind, was not an influence that frightened him into it. It is not a fright. It is a rational deduction. And for all the purposes of judgment on this particular question, he is as sober as he ever was. And as he did not come here by a fright, so neither does it require that sort of influence to urge him on, till he shall consent and submit to the terms of the Gospel. He needs only—and that surely he does need—an *accumulation* of the same class of reasons, which have already quickened his conscience, and roused it to its proper office. But any efforts, that should quiet his conscience, would involve the fearful responsibility of 'healing his hurt slightly.'

Is it said, the Gospel should be preached to him?—And what is meant by this?—Is it supposed, that all this while he is ignorant of the Gospel?—that he never heard 'that Jesus Christ came into the world to save sinners?'— It is his knowledge of the Gospel, in connexion with the law, which has induced this state of mind. He has not unlikely been educated from his cradle, not only in the cardinal doctrines, but in the minutest elements of Christianity. And if his minister has been faithful, he has no ignorance of this kind to plead in extenuation of the guilt of his unbelief. He is not uninformed of the great atoning sacrifice. The difficulty lies somewhere else. It is within him. It is his perverseness. He is wicked against God. He will not consent to be saved in the way, which God has revealed ; which has been well defined, and incessantly declared to him.

But it is said,—the Gospel brings consolation. On what condition?—And to whom ?—For myself, I confess, I have yet to learn, that there is a single element in the Gospel, which can reasonably console an impenitent sinner—an unbeliever. So long as this is his character, ' the wrath of God *abideth* on him.' I have yet to learn, that in the whole range of Evangelical doctrine, there can be found one consideration, which does not aggravate his guilt. How, then, can he be consoled, except by blinding his eyes, and keeping him ignorant?—I wish always to be understood, as distinguishing between the *encouragements*, which the Gospel holds out to inquiring sinners, and the consolations proper to Christian hope.

The Gospel *encourages* an anxious, inquiring sinner, just so far as he is honest, and when he is prepared to profit by it. But a Gospel sinned against is a *law*, and the most fearful law of condemnation. And every successive hour of the sinner's life, until the moment of his repentance, multiplies the guilt of violating that law. The more he knows, and the better he understands the Gospel,—until he has experienced its pardoning mercy in consequence of his repentance,—the more occasion of inquietude has he. Yes, certainly, and by all means preach the Gospel—and the whole Gospel.

I do not allow, that I am making an argument with those, who mean nothing more by conversion, than a renunciation of Paganism, or any form of false religion, and an acknowledgment of Christianity, as the only true religion. I have heard such preaching in England,—I have heard it in America. But such men are themselves Pagans, and need the very conversion which they preach. Certainly such a supposition would be their best apology. But I assume, that conversion is a radical change of the heart, involving the repentance of the sinner and the transforming power of the Holy Ghost, however enlightened he may have been in the knowledge, and however firmly established in a speculative belief, of Christianity—however pure his charac-

ter before the world, and however exact his obedience of the second table of the Decalogue.
And it is the preaching most likely to induce
this change instrumentally, of which I am now
speaking.

But I intended to say more to defend this
kind of preaching from the charge of being *terrific.* I am no friend of declamatory preaching,
nor of the employment of a factitious imagery of
the wrath of God, and the world of woe, the
effect of which is merely to astound people's
nerves. Nor would I, on proper occasions,
withhold an iota of the denunciations of the
Bible, against the impenitent,—neither would I
explain away the force of that imagery of the
Bible, which depicts the condition of the lost.
But that kind of preaching, to which I allude,
has little, or no relation to exhibitions of this
sort; the relation certainly is very remote. But
it is such an exhibition of Divine truth, as
tends to convince the impenitent sinner, not
alone, nor principally, of the fearful doom of
original law against him; but rather and more
especially, of his ingratitude, of his baseness, of
his inexcusable fault, and of his exceeding,
damning guilt, for sinning against the Gospel.

And this latter impression should be so deeply laid in the soul, so firmly riveted on the conscience, as if possible to swallow up the former—that the sinner might well nigh forget that he is going to hell, in the absorptions of that other element of conviction, that he has sinned against such a holy God, and so long rejected such a compassionate Saviour. He should be made to feel, that if he deserves hell for his transgressions of the law, he deserves more than hell for his contempts of the Gospel. Of course such preaching implies a presentation of the Gospel, in all its fulness. It is not to be taken for granted, that the sinner involved in such distress, does not understand the Gospel, and needs it to be preached to him. It is because it *has* been preached to him, and because he *does* understand it. It is not simply because his minister has stood up before him, clothed in the terrors of Sinai; but rather, and especially, because his minister has opened to his vision all the tenderness of a dying Redeemer. It is not the fear of punishment, that agitates his bosom—it is the pangs of remorse. He has been *ungrateful,* and now to him ingratitude, of all others, is his crying sin—his weighty, soul-oppressing guilt.

And I will not take the trouble to affirm—that such preaching is not only the tenderest, but the most effectual motive to repentance. The sinner, awakened by such means, finds himself already at the foot of the Cross. And his greatest hesitation, not unlikely, will arise from the sense of his unworthiness, the baseness of his ingratitude, the shame of his guilt. But still he hesitates—he demurs—he refuses. He disobeys God by not repenting; he dishonours Christ by not believing. He seems near the point of compliance—of submission. But still he maintains the integrity of his perverseness. And now shall he be driven from his last hold—his trembling grasp of some forbidden love—of anything but God and Christ? Or, shall he be fostered and strengthened in it?—Shall he be told—now you have got far enough?—Now you are safe? It is not a trifling change, when the sinner resigns the world, and embraces the Saviour. And according to the phenomena of mind, as exhibited in revivals, this change is ordinarily made manifest to the subject of it, by an influence, which is supposed to be from above—from the Holy Spirit. And while nothing of the Gospel is withheld, it is not considered, that its consolations can be legitimately appropriated by an impenitent sinner. And if it is the office of the Holy Spirit to seal pardon upon the conscience, it is an assumption of Divine prerogative for man to attempt it. And facts, developed in revivals of religion, and also in insulated conversions, prove that it is unnecessary.

And this, generally (that is, the remarks of these few pages), is what I mean by my definition of revival-preaching in the United States:—
That it is a studious effort to combine the cardinal principles of original and evangelical law, and a persevering application of those principles, in their various Scriptural forms, through the understanding and reason, to the consciences of impenitent sinners—until they come to repentance.—Until they come to repentance. It is pressing their consciences with all the variety of truth, that flows from these two sources. Nor is it considered expedient, or suitable, to change this mode of treatment, *until* the object in view be attained—*until* there is evidence of repentance.

The rule, however it may be understood, is general. It is not indispensable, it is impossible, that it should be applied invariably in any particular and definite form—in any set phrase of speech. As the physician has the whole *materia medica* under his hand, from which to select ingredients, according to his best discretion, for the treatment of the various forms, under which physical disease is developed, taking the symptoms as an indication of what is wanted; so has the minister of Christ the whole range of the Bible—of original and evangelical law—from which to select his topics and his arguments to the consciences of impenitent sinners. And as a prudent and skilful physician never thinks himself justified in administering *tonics*, before he has subdued and eradicated the disease, with which he has to contend,—so neither can the prudent and skilful minister lawfully proceed to build up the hopes of the sinner, while his sin is unsubdued—while the disease still maintains its empire in the heart, lurks and rankles in the vitals of his moral constitution, and will only be nourished by consolations unseasonably administered.

Still, however, it is not to be denied, that as the physician of the body deems it prudent to know all the peculiarities of the physical condition and temperament of his patient, to ascertain the particular form of disease, by which he is affected, and to consult all its symptoms, so that he may prescribe and administer most effectually, commending his patient to a careful and tender nursing;—so is it prudent for the minister of religion, (who is always supposed to know the nature of the disease, with which he has to contend,) to consult all the peculiarities of moral temperament, which come under his treatment, and to observe their symptoms; to ascertain the particular forms, (I do not mean by *auricular confession*) under which the disease of sin has been developed, in the individual persons, that may be the subjects of his advice, and to be guided in his administrations by all the knowledge of which he is lawfully possessed. There can be no question, that in the treatment of individual minds, there must be a discretion of this sort. But he has his principles to guide him. As in the former profession, there is *the theory and the practice;* so in the latter, there is *the doctrine and its application.* The *minister* must not administer *tonics,* while the disease is in full power.

I have admitted in a former chapter, under a brief notice of this topic, that when morbid affections of mind present themselves, arising from physical causes, such minds form an exception to the general rule. All peculiar cases are of course to be left in the discretion, and imposed on the responsibility of the wise and discerning minister—*so*, that he wins them to Christ.

There is a pulpit vice, (and the pulpit has its vices,) allied to this topic, and unfriendly to this kind of preaching, and a great obstacle to revivals, which owes its origin to an unfortunate popular demand. It is this: that every religious service, and every sermon must have a certain kind of *completeness*. It allows no discretion to the minister. I do not speak, as to the order of public services. For, there can be no question, but they should be uniform—those, I mean, that are ordinary and stated. But I refer to the impression, which the minister, acquainted with the state of his congregation, may think it expedient to endeavour to leave upon them, from time to time, with a view to the greatest good—with a view, we will say, to a revival.

For the sake of illustration, take an individual mind. It is evident, that a minister needs to be intimately acquainted with the character, temper, degree of religious knowledge, and present state of that mind, in order to treat it most advantageously in his official capacity. His ignorance might possibly be the occasion of losing all his labour. He needs such acquaintance, that he may know what to say, how to say it, and where to stop. It is true, that there are certain common characteristics of every mind, and certain general religious considerations, of almost universal application. But we are now speaking of advantages for the attainment of the greatest good, to a given state of mind.

It is true also, that individual communities do not differ so much as individual minds. But still they differ. And every community is itself constantly developing new features. And for the main purposes of a pastor's treatment of that portion of the public mind, committed to his charge, if he desires a revival, he may regard it generally as an *unity*. And he, if anybody, should know the general state of that public mind. And he should prayerfully devise his plan of treatment.

This, if I mistake not, is a great secret of revival-ministers in the United States. They endeavour to ascertain generally and particularly, as far as possible, the character and temper of the community. Their main object, of course, is, to awaken religious inquiry, and to secure individual instances of deep religious concern. And when they address the public mind in mass, they seek to make a particular impression, and then watch and cultivate that impression, both in public and in private. They devise their system of preaching, and adapt it to the exigencies of the public mind, for the time being, varying as symptoms vary, and watching the successive developements of the general feeling, maintaining scrupulously that leading character, which I have defined. They do not sacrifice this object for the sake of having a *complete* sermon—that should be such in the eyes of a critic, or in popular demand. The Bible, as a text book, opens an infinitely various field, and they can never be at a loss to find topics and thoughts there to answer their purpose. If they wish for a revival, they must preach, so as to make Christians go home and pray, and impenitent sinners go home and weep. And when, by the blessing of God, they observe an unusual solemnity on the public mind, they must still reat it as an *unity*, in all their public ministrations,—in some such manner, as they would treat an individual inquiring sinner: seek to augment that solemnity. The topics of the pulpit should be selected, and the manner of treating them all be resolved on, for this single purpose. And so with all extraordinary measures, ' in season or out of season,' in public or in private. It should be an object to dismiss every religious assembly under such impressions, as that the people may go away, not to compliment the preacher, but to find fault with themselves, and retire to their closets. And such effects are hopeful symptoms of a revival. But, to have awakened seriousness in a congregation, in the progress of a sermon, and then to be obliged by popular demand to turn and do it all away, by some very kind and gracious words, is not only a sad state of things, but a sacrifice of ministerial fidelity. It is an insuperable obstacle to the conducting forward of the public mind to the condition of a revival.

It is equally erroneous in judgment, it is unphilosophical, (and *because* it is unphilosophical,) to suppose,—that the whole scope of Christianity should be embodied in every sermon, or as much of it, as can be conveniently crowded in. Neither an individual mind, nor the public mind of a congregation, is sufficiently capacious to receive so much matter at any one time, or to make a profitable improvement of it. It only multiplies the impressions, and consequently weakens them, just in proportion to their number. Resolve an elementary power, either in the physical, or moral world—and the single and separate action of the several influences, thus multiplied, will be diminished in force, in proportion to the number of ramifications. It is *some one grand impression*, that should be sought after at any one time, and every thought, for the time being, should be made to minister to that end. Nothing should be suffered to come in, that might divert the attention, and detract from the power of that impression. Every mind, the whole community, should retire under all its weight, that it may ring in their ears, follow them into their retreats, give character to their night visions—that when they think of their minister, or meet him, they may feel as if he knew their hearts.

The truth is,—that the Gospel, in its principal and prime elements, is before every Christian community. And there is not probably a man in Christendom, who is not fully informed of this great historical fact: that Jesus Christ, the Son of God, came into the world to save sinners. Much more is the pastor of a Christian congregation to know, that his own hearers are well certified of this. If they are not, it must be his own fault. And if he has been in any tolerable degree faithful—if he has been accustomed to read and expound the Bible to his people, from time to time, and from year to year, they must be supposed to have a general knowledge of the capital and leading principles of Christianity. Indeed, it is fair to conclude, that this is the ordinary condition of Christian communities. But the great difficulty, the deplorable fact is, that with all this information, with all this knowledge, in general and in particular, sinners do not repent. Some of the best theologians * are the greatest sinners—if not most flagitious in their lives, yet most guilty in the sight of God for their sin against knowledge. Such minds do not so much need information, as feeling. The want of feeling is the ordinary,

---

* For such there are in every well-educated Christian congregation, and yet unconverted.

the grand defect. In every Christian land, and in every particular community, the knowledge of divine truth is greatly in advance of a conviction of it on the heart—on the conscience. Is it not prudent therefore, is it not duty, to labour to supply this defect, by seeking the revival of vital religion? As the main object of the Gospel is to save sinners, the main object of its ministrations should be to *convert* sinners. And that method of preaching, which is ordinarily most successful in the attainment of this end— in awakening religious concern in the minds of individuals, and in the mind of a community, and bringing sinners to repentance—is at least worthy of respect—worthy of grave consideration. For after all, if the word of God does not come ' in power,' it comes to little purpose.

Perhaps, the entire character of that kind of preaching, which I have here attempted to define, and which has been most successful in promoting American revivals, might be expressed in this single sentence : the *earnest* preaching of the law and Gospel—*so earnest,* that the people cannot fail to feel that the preachers *are* in earnest.

As I said in the beginning of this chapter,

that it was out of my original plan; so I beg leave to conclude with the expression of a hope, that I shall not be deemed arrogant for anything I have advanced in it. And if in anything I have not given a fair presentation, it is only because the impressions of my opportunities of observation have deceived me. It may, perhaps, be thought, that I might have stated facts, without obtruding and defending opinions. But I have already stated, as my apology for introducing this chapter, that it was suggested and advised under an apprehension, that some previous naked statements of this sort might be misunderstood.

CHAPTER XIV.

TO BRITISH CHRISTIANS.

HAVING executed all, and more than all, that I contemplated, when I sat down to this little work, I am unwilling—(considering the circumstances under which it comes into being, and the subject of which it treats, and my own peculiar relation to those for whom it has been written)—to conclude without a word of direct address to British Christians—to all who may feel sufficient interest to read these pages. As I reserve for the Introduction my apology for this obtrusion upon their attention, I would simply remark here, that nothing was farther from my thoughts, than a discharge of an office of this kind, until it seemed to be forced upon me by unanticipated Providential occurrences. And having gone thus far, I feel too much interest, to dismiss the subject, without expressing some feelings, which could not conveniently be embodied in the previous discussions.

The relations subsisting between Great

Britain and the United States, and their relations to the world, are, as all must admit, of an interesting nature, and of a momentous character. And while it is proper for Christians, for the Church, as such, to leave the management of political concerns to those who are ordained to these offices, praying that the two nations may ever cultivate and maintain peace, it cannot be otherwise than pleasant to regard the opportunities, which Providence is affording, for frequent and friendly intercourse, and for the most intimate alliances between the Christian subjects of the two empires. And I need not undertake to prove the satisfaction and importance of such intercourse and such friendships. And as it is in the power of Great Britain and the United States, from their political importance and influence, to do much for the political and general welfare of mankind ; so is it in the power of Christians of the two nations, by a concerted and combined influence, to make a far greater impression upon the world for religious objects, than by separate action. Christianity is a religion of sympathy. It is eminently social. And all subjects of its thorough influences acquire an incalculable moral power by intercourse and fellowship. It imparts an inappreciable energy to their enterprise. Who can calculate the impulse of increased moral power, which has been imparted to the cause of Christianity, within a generation past, by the union of Christians, in Bible, Missionary, Tract, and other religious and benevolent Associations?—Who, sitting upon the stage, or making one of the vast assemblies convened to celebrate the anniversaries of these institutions, has not felt his sectarian prejudices melting down, his heart filling and beating with love to mankind, in a degree and with a purity unknown before, his affections assimilating with those who are called by a different name, until he begins to feel ' how pleasant it is for brethren to dwell together in unity;'—until, as John Summerfield said, (himself a native of these realms, a very child of Whitfield, a pattern of meekness and Christian purity, and almost unrivalled for the simplicity and power of his eloquence—the last time he ever opened his lips in public, and on one of these occasions, which happened to be the formation of the American Tract Society)—until, as that young man said, on that occasion,—' The anointing oil of Christian fellow ship, like that of Aaron's consecration, poured upon the head, is felt trickling down over the whole frame, seen distilling from the fingers, and realized to be diffusing its sweet and grateful fragrance throughout all the region?'—And who has not felt, in retiring from these great religious festivals, that he must make other and newer sacrifices for the peace of the Church—that it is profane and sacrilegious to invade a brother's rights of conscience—that he must ' work while the day lasts' with those who together with him are devoted to the interests of a common religion—that he must henceforth offer up all his prayers and bend all his energies, in conjunction with his brethren throughout the world, for the complete establishment and last triumphs of Christianity?

And if such are the social influences of the union of Christians of different sects, in the same country, for the catholic purposes of their religion—and if the secret of this moral effect lies vested in that enlargement of mind and of feeling, which such associations naturally produce—as doubtless it does—then clearly, the wider, the more extended the sympathy, the greater the benefit. Let Christians of different nations feel, that to them 'there is one Lord, one faith, one baptism'—that they are one family—and that they are interested in and pledged to a common cause. Should it not be assumed, that the sympathies of Christianity are *catholic*, not only by Divine purpose, but in their very nature?—And consequently, that it is impossible, they should ever have their intended, most thorough and purifying influence, but by the operation of this principle? —The design and scope of Christianity embrace nothing less, than the subjugation of the world to Jesus Christ. And that Christian, who thinks or prays for anything less, who lays his plans for anything short—thinks, and prays, and labours, so far, under the influence of a contracted mind. But we have not been so taught by Jesus Christ. We ought ' not so to have learned Christ.'

It is to be confessed in favour of British Christians, that they have led the way, as an example for the Christian world, in their devices and labours for the most enlarged Christian enterprise. And American Christians, catching the same spirit from their brethren in this land of their fathers, have followed quickly in their train. They have not thought it worthy to decline imitation, but have cheerfully and unanimously come here for the patterns of their grand benevolent institutions, and are ready to confess themselves obliged for these important and interesting facilities, framed at their hands. And the subsequent friendly correspondence which has been maintained, the Christian fellowship and sympathy which have been cherished and fostered between kindred benevolent institutions in England and the United States, have contributed immeasurably to that healthful excitement and energy, which originated them, and which conducts them onward in their career of triumphant exploits. And now, so far as I know, (and I trust I am not deceived in this impression,) it has got to be an acknowledged and practical principle—and it is certainly a wise one—to be willing to be indebted to any quarter for an important and useful suggestion. If any new principle is first developed by the success of actual experiment in England, in the management of these institutions, it is respected and applied in the United States. If the same thing occurs there, it is equally respected here. And this is as it should be. It is the best practical economy of the Christian hosts.

Now, it has occurred in the Providence of God, that a notable series of dispensations has seemed to characterize extended portions of the religious world in the United States, more or less for a hundred years, but especially during the present generation, which does not seem to be so well understood on this side of the Atlantic—dispensations of a somewhat novel character, powerfully affecting the public mind, exciting religious inquiry to an uncommon degree, issuing in the more rapid and multiplied conversion of sinners, extending the pale of the church, prompting extraordinary religious efforts, and crowning those efforts with great success. And these dispensations claim and are believed, by the Christian communities, among which they have occurred, to have their origin in extraordinary effusions of the Holy Spirit. And although a different opinion has sometimes been formed and expressed, by professing Christians, and ministers even, who have either lived remote from the scenes, or have wanted opportunities of observation adequate to decide upon their character, or allowed themselves to be influenced by prejudice—yet those Christians and those ministers, who have providentially been planted in the midst of these scenes, and who have been compelled to have to do them, ordinarily have but one mind, one impression, and that undoubting, as to their being the genuine fruits of the operation of the Spirit of God. They could not, indeed, as philosophers, account for them by any other cause. They see the human mind acted upon in ways and forms, and under circumstances, and in so many instances, so utterly inexplicable by the common laws of social influence, or by any common effects of mental introversion, or by the combined influences of these two causes, even under all the energy of the most powerful concentration of religious truth, —that they must stand embarrassed and confounded, independent of some other solution. And as the effect is good—as there is a manifest amendment of heart and life in consequence—a great change and rich fruit—honourable to God,—and inasmuch as the Bible predicts and asserts an influence of this sort distinctly and prominently, and propounds it as the only efficient power, adequate for the renovation of the world, and designed for this very purpose,—it is not only natural, but reasonable (philosophical, if needs be) to resolve the great question, by a reference to this great and Almighty Power. And so it stands resolved, in the estimation of the most sober, the most discreet, and the best of men—men, standing highest in the State, as well as in the church—private Christians and ministers. And if a canvass of the names entertaining this opinion were to be made, their comparative weight estimated, and their opportunities of observation considered—the question of the validity, of the genuineness, of the importance, and usefulness of American revivals of religion, so far as human judgment is to be respected, might in all prudence be considered as settled. I cannot in honesty imagine, that any testimony can be brought worthy to invalidate such a verdict —or that any considerable number of persons can be found, of notorious celebrity for their pure and high devotion to Christian enterprise, and for catholic feeling, who would be willing to risk their reputation before the world, in a contradiction of this statement.

Thus, then, stands the case:—these dispensations of Providence have been in train, before the world, for one hundred years,—they have made a great impression upon the communities where they have occurred, and given them a marked character—they have out-lived disaster and prevailed against opposition—they have spread and been multiplied—they have worked surprising transformations for the better, not only in individual persons, but in communities —they have found and made their subjects out of all ranks, from the lowest to the highest conditions of society—until finally, by their more rapid progress and more extensive influence, they have imposed themselves upon the attention of the Christian world. They claim to be of God. And the rule, given by the Divine author of our religion : ' By their fruits ye shall know them,'—may be applied here under the most rigid scrutiny, and they will grow brighter and brighter.

And this is the high claim, under which, with all humility, so far as my own endeavours are concerned, I presume to solicit the candid attention of British Christians, to the great subject of this little volume. That portion of the religious history of the United States, comprehended under this review and in these discussions, is a series of important and interesting facts. And if indeed they are the effect of the special out-pourings of the Spirit of God, as they certainly seem to be, do they not promise something for the world?—Ought not the Christian world, now looking and waiting for some extraordinary interpositions of Providence,—having themselves instituted extraordinary measures, framed and put in operation extraordinary machinery, and actually embarked in extraordinary enterprises —ought they not to give so much of their attention to this extraordinary feature of the religious world, as may enable them in all candour to determine its character? And is not something of this kind consistent with the expectations of the age?—consistent with prophecy?—and in perfect coincidence with one of the most cardinal and most prominent doctrines of Revelation?—And is it not also evident, that independent of some such dispensations, the progress of Christianity must remain in check, and worldliness and practical irreligion for ever hold the vantage-ground?—The simple question seems to be,—are Christians of the present day really, heartily, and fervently desirous of the complete establishment and most thorough sway of their religion, in the hearts of men?—And if so, will they not hail every symptom of such revival of religion, as may seem to promise the more speedy attainment of this end?

I say, then, to all British Christians—Yonder, on the American shores, and on the American continent, *are some such symptoms.* *There* God is doing a work, which may well claim the grave consideration of the Christian world, and inspire them with hope. And it is the proper *character* of this work, without attempting the detail of its history, which it has been the principal aim of this volume to develope.

It will doubtless be confessed, that Christians throughout the world are one family, have one common cause, and being strangers and pilgrims on the earth, are seeking another and a common country, in a better world. As Christians they have no country here. ' The field is the world,' and the world is the field of their enterprise. Every advantage gained, in whatever part of the globe, is an advantage to the common interest, whether on pagan ground, or in a Christian land. And we ought doubtless to welcome such intelligence, with gratitude to God, whether it comes from the antipodes, or from a neighbouring country, or whether it springs up at our own doors. And I beg here to acknowledge, that it has been exceedingly grateful to my feelings, as an American, to witness, as I have uniformly witnessed, the exemplification of this spirit among Christians in England, in relation to those distinguished favours of the Head of the Church, bestowed upon my native country, which make the subject of this volume. This kind and catholic spirit, demonstrated in so many forms, (and I am happy to say, that I have never yet met with an exception to it) has encouraged me to speak with great freedom and openness. I could indeed have avoided some of those discussions, which perhaps may be deemed by some of a delicate nature, had I not conceived them of real and practical importance —too important and too relevant to the general subject, to be passed over without apparent loss. I have given such credit to Christians in England, as to be fully persuaded, that they will listen to a presentation of this great and interesting subject by an American, with all the candour which could reasonably be asked—especially when it is done at their own solicitation—not, indeed, by official appointment, but at the instance of numerous and respectable individuals, and to meet what would seem to be a general demand. Stranger as I am in this land of my fathers, and belonging only to a scion cut off from this original stock, and transplanted into a distant region, I cannot be supposed a competent judge of the comparative state of religion here. Whether that scion has flourished better in its new soil, and imbibed a more healthful influence from another climate, and whether it is growing up into more beautiful forms, and bearing more abundant and richer fruit, than the original plant—can better be decided by those, who know how things are here, when they have received sufficient testimony of the condition and prospects of their own transatlantic progeny. For, we are *all* children of the same ancestry. It would be ungracious in us, Americans, not to respect and venerate those, from whom we have sprung. And we are happy to have received so many proofs of a fraternal regard among the descendants of a common stock. And we come to tell them, at their own condescending request, how God hath prospered us. Even if we look at the political relations of the two countries, they are friendly, and we hope ever will be. As fellow-*Christians*, (and it is as such we now speak,—none else will be interested in this subject,) we confide fully, and without distrust. There cannot be foundation for any other rivalship, than ' to provoke one another to love and good works,' to all possible excellence in Christian purity and Christian enterprise.

And now may the Great Head of the Church smile upon this feeble effort, and cause it to be well received among those, for whose information it has been undertaken, and to whom it is now humbly submitted—with this additional and earnest prayer :—That it may contribute to the honour of Jesus Christ, and to the furtherance of his cause.

THE END.